DATE LOANED SLIP
Books due in two weeks from last date

WITHDRAWN

ACROSS ASIA ON A BICYCLE

THROUGH WESTERN CHINA IN LIGHT MARCHING ORDER.

ACROSS ASIA ON A BICYCLE

THE JOURNEY OF TWO AMERICAN STUDENTS
FROM CONSTANTINOPLE TO PEKING

BY

THOMAS GASKELL ALLEN, Jr.
AND
WILLIAM LEWIS SACHTLEBEN

NEW YORK
THE CENTURY CO.
1894

Copyright, 1894, by
THE CENTURY CO.

All rights reserved.

THE DE VINNE PRESS.

TO

THOSE AT HOME

WHOSE THOUGHTS AND
WISHES WERE EVER
WITH US IN OUR
WANDERINGS

PREFACE

This volume is made up of a series of sketches describing the most interesting part of a bicycle journey around the world,—our ride across Asia. We were actuated by no desire to make a "record" in bicycle travel, although we covered 15,044 miles on the wheel, the longest continuous land journey ever made around the world.

The day after we were graduated at Washington University, St. Louis, Mo., we left for New York. Thence we sailed for Liverpool on June 23, 1890. Just three years afterward, lacking twenty days, we rolled into New York on our wheels, having "put a girdle round the earth."

Our bicycling experience began at Liverpool. After following many of the beaten lines of travel in the British Isles we arrived in London, where we formed our plans for traveling across Europe, Asia, and America. The most dangerous regions to be traversed in such a journey, we were told, were western China, the Desert of Gobi, and central China. Never since the days of Marco Polo had a European traveler succeeded in crossing the Chinese empire from the west to Peking.

Crossing the Channel, we rode through Normandy to Paris, across the lowlands of western France to Bordeaux, eastward over the Lesser Alps to Marseilles, and along the Riviera into Italy. After visiting every important city on the peninsula, we left Italy at Brindisi on the last day of 1890 for Corfu, in Greece. Thence we traveled to Patras, proceeding along the Corinthian Gulf to Athens, where we passed the winter. We went to Constantinople by vessel in the spring, crossed the Bosporus in April, and began the long journey described in the following pages. When we had finally completed our travels in the Flowery Kingdom, we sailed from Shanghai for Japan. Thence we voyaged to San Francisco, where we arrived on Christmas night, 1892. Three weeks later we resumed our bicycles and wheeled by way of Arizona, New Mexico, and Texas to New York.

During all of this journey we never employed the services of guides or interpreters. We were compelled, therefore, to learn a little of the language of every country through which we passed. Our independence in this regard increased, perhaps, the hardships of the journey, but certainly contributed much toward the object we sought — a close acquaintance with strange peoples.

During our travels we took more than two thousand five hundred photographs, selections from which are reproduced in the illustrations of this volume.

CONTENTS

		PAGE
I.	BEYOND THE BOSPORUS	1
II.	THE ASCENT OF MOUNT ARARAT . . .	43
III.	THROUGH PERSIA TO SAMARKAND . . .	83
IV.	THE JOURNEY FROM SAMARKAND TO KULDJA .	115
V.	OVER THE GOBI DESERT AND THROUGH THE WESTERN GATE OF THE GREAT WALL . . .	149
VI.	AN INTERVIEW WITH THE PRIME MINISTER OF CHINA	207

ACROSS ASIA ON A BICYCLE

ACROSS ASIA ON A BICYCLE

THE JOURNEY OF TWO AMERICAN STUDENTS FROM CONSTANTINOPLE TO PEKING

I

BEYOND THE BOSPORUS

ON a morning early in April the little steamer conveying us across from Stamboul touched the wharf at Haider Pasha. Amid the rabble of Greeks, Armenians, Turks, and Italians we trundled our bicycles across the gang-plank, which for us was the threshold of Asia, the beginning of an inland journey of seven thousand miles from the Bosporus to the Pacific. Through the morning fog which enveloped the shipping in the Golden Horn, the "stars and stripes" at a single masthead were waving farewell to two American students fresh from college who had nerved themselves for nearly two years of separation from the comforts of western civilization.

Our guide to the road to Ismid was the little twelve-year-old son of an Armenian doctor, whose guests we had been during our sojourn in Stamboul. He trotted for some distance by our side, and then, pressing our hands in both of his, he said with childlike sincerity: "I hope God will take care of you"; for he was possessed with the thought popular among Armenians, of pillages and massacres by marauding brigands.

The idea of a trip around the world had been conceived by us as a practical finish to a theoretical education; and the bicycle feature was adopted merely as a means to that end. On reaching London we had formed the plan of penetrating the heart of the Asiatic continent, instead of skirting its more civilized coast-line. For a passport and other credentials necessary in journeying through Russia and Central Asia we had been advised to make application to the Czar's representative on our arrival at Teheran, as we would enter the Russian dominions from Persia; and to that end the Russian minister in London had provided us with a letter of introduction. In London the secretary of the Chinese legation, a Scotchman, had assisted us in mapping out a possible route across the Celestial empire, although he endeavored, from the very start, to dissuade us from our purpose. Application had then been made to the Chinese minister himself for the necessary passport. The reply we received, though courteous, smacked strongly of reproof. "Western China," he said, "is overrun with lawless bands, and the people themselves are very much averse to foreigners. Your extraordinary mode of locomotion would subject you to annoyance, if not to positive danger, at the hands of a people who are naturally curious and superstitious. However," he added, after some reflection, "if your minister makes a request for a passport we will see what can be done. The most I can do will be to ask for you the protection and assistance of the officials only; for the people themselves I cannot answer. If you go into that country you do so at your own risk." Minister Lincoln was sitting in his private office when we called the next morning at the American legation. He listened to the recital of our plans, got down the huge atlas from his bookcase, and went over with us the route we proposed to follow. He did not regard the undertaking as feasible, and apprehended that, if he should give his official assistance, he would, in a measure, be responsible for the result if it should prove unhappy. When assured of the consent of our parents, and of our determination to make the attempt at all hazards, he picked up his pen and began a letter to the Chinese minister, remarking as he finished reading it to us, "I would much rather not have written it." The documents received from the Chinese minister in response to Mr. Lincoln's letter proved to be indispensable when, a year and a half later, we left the last outpost of western civilization and plunged into the Gobi desert. When we had paid a final visit to the Persian minister in London, who had asked to see our bicycles and their baggage equipments, he signified his intention of writing in our behalf to friends in Teheran; and to that capital, after cycling through Europe, we were now actually *en route*.

Since the opening of the Trans-Bosporus Railway, the wagon-road to Ismid, and even the Angora military highway beyond, have fallen rapidly into disrepair. In April they were almost impassable for the wheel, so that for the greater part of the way we were obliged to take to the track. Like the railway skirting the Italian Riviera, and the Patras-Athens line along the Saronic Gulf, this Trans-Bosporus road for a great distance scarps and tunnels the cliffs along the Gulf of Ismid, and sometimes runs so close to the water's edge that the puffing of the *kara vapor* or

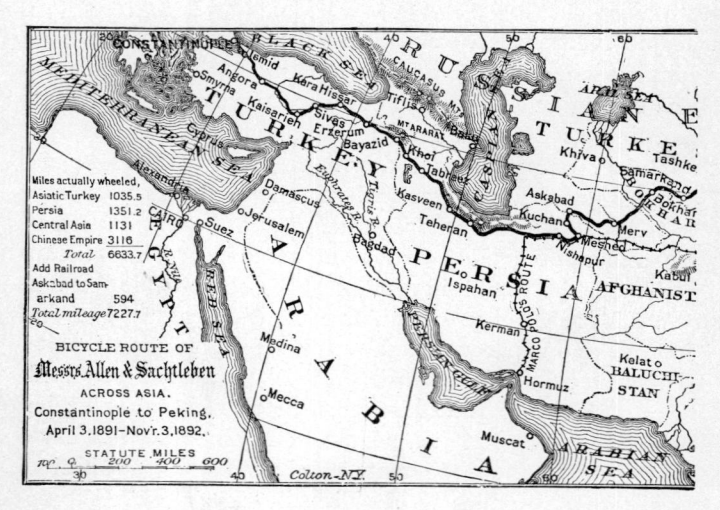

Miles actually wheeled,
Asiatic Turkey 1035.5
Persia   1351.2
Central Asia 1131
Chinese Empire 3116
 Total   6633.7
Add Railroad
Askabad to Samarkand 594
Total mileage 7227.7

BICYCLE ROUTE OF
Messrs. Allen & Sachtleben
ACROSS ASIA.
Constantinople to Peking,
April 3, 1891–Nov'r. 3, 1892.

"land steamer," as the Turks call it, is drowned by the roaring breakers. The country between Scutari and Ismid surpasses in agricultural advantages any part of Asiatic Turkey through which we passed. Its fertile soil, and the luxuriant vegetation it supports, are, as we afterward learned, in striking contrast with the sterile plateaus and mountains of the interior, many parts of which are as desolate as the deserts of Arabia. In area, Asia Minor equals France, but the water-supply of its rivers is only one third.

One of the principal agents in the work of transforming Asia Minor is the railroad, to which the natives have taken with unusual readiness. The locomotive is already competing with the hundred and sixty thousand camels employed in the peninsula caravan-trade. At Geiveh, the last station on the Trans-Bosporus Railway, where we left the track to follow the Angora highway, the "ships of the desert" are beginning to transfer their cargoes to the "land steamer," instead of continuing on as in former days to the Bosporus.

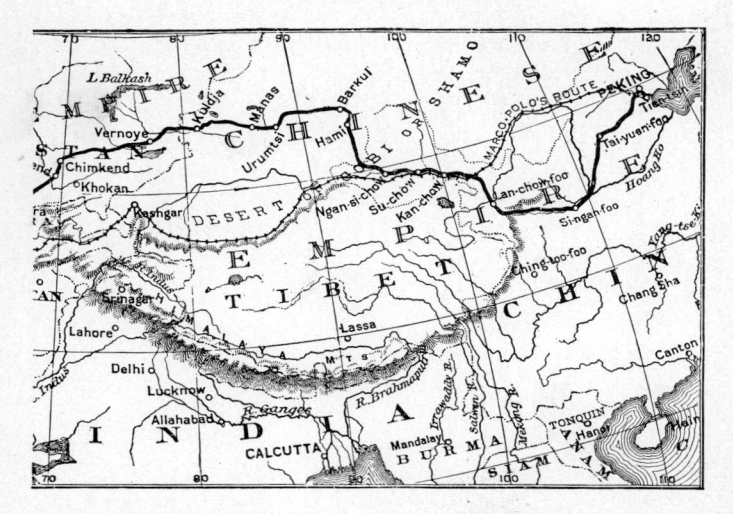

The Trans-Bosporus line, in the year of our visit, was being built and operated by a German company, under the direct patronage of the Sultan. We ventured to ask some natives if they thought the Sultan had sufficient funds to consummate so gigantic a scheme, and they replied, with the deepest reverence: "God has given the Padishah much property and power, and certainly he must give him enough money to utilize it."

A week's cycling from the Bosporus brought us beyond the Allah Dagh mountains, among the barren, variegated hills that skirt the Angora plateau. We had already passed through Ismid, the ancient Nicomedia and capital of Diocletian; and had left behind us the heavily timbered valley of the Sakaria, upon whose banks the "Freebooter of the Bithynian hills" settled with his four hundred tents and laid the foundation of the Ottoman empire. Since leaving Geiveh we had been attended by a mounted guard, or *zaptieh*, who was sometimes forced upon us by the authorities in their anxiety to carry out the wishes expressed in the letters of the Grand Vizir. On emerging from the door of an inn we frequently found this unex-

THE DONKEY BOYS INSPECT THE "DEVIL'S CARRIAGE."

pected guard waiting with a Winchester rifle swung over his shoulder, and a fleet steed standing by his side. Immediately on our appearance he would swing into the saddle and charge through the assembled rabble. Away we would go at a rapid pace down the streets of the town or village, to the utter amazement of the natives and the great satisfaction of our vainglorious zaptieh. As long as his horse was fresh, or until we were out of sight of the village, he would urge us on with cries of "Gellcha-buk" ("Come on, ride fast"). When a bad piece of road or a steep ascent forced us to dismount he would bring his horse to a walk, roll a cigarette, and draw invidious comparisons between our steeds. His tone, however, changed when we reached a decline or long stretch of reasonably good road. Then he would cut across country to head us off, or shout after us at the top of his voice, "Yavash-yavash" ("Slowly, slowly"). On the whole we found them good-natured and companionable fellows, notwithstanding their interest in *baksheesh* which we were compelled at last, in self-defense, to fix at one piaster an hour. We frequently shared with them our frugal, and even scanty meals; and in turn they assisted us in our purchases and arrangements for lodgings, for their word, we found, was with the common people an almost unwritten law. Then, too, they were of great assistance in crossing streams where the depth would have necessitated the stripping of garments; although their fiery little steeds sometimes objected to having an extra rider astride their haunches, and a bicycle across their shoulders. They seized every opportunity to impress us with the necessity of being accompanied by a government representative. In some lonely portion of the road, or in the suggestive stillness of an evening twilight, our Turkish Don Quixote would sometimes cast mysterious glances around him, take his Winchester from his shoulder, and throwing it across the pommel of his saddle, charge ahead to meet the imaginary enemy. But we were more harmful than harmed, for, despite our most vigilant care, the bicycles were sometimes the occasion of a stampede or runaway among the caravans and teams along the highway, and

HELPING A TURK WHOSE HORSES RAN AWAY AT SIGHT OF OUR BICYCLES.

we frequently assisted in replacing the loads thus upset. On such occasions our pretentious cavalier would remain on his horse, smoking his cigarette and smiling disdainfully.

It was in the company of one of these military champions that we emerged on the morning of April 12 upon the plateau of Angora. On the spring pasture were feeding several flocks of the famous Angora goats, and the *karamanli* or fat-tailed sheep, tended by the Yurak shepherds and their half-wild and monstrous collies, whose half-savage nature fits them to cope with the jackals which infest the country. The shepherds did not check their sudden onslaught upon us until we were pressed to very close quarters, and had drawn our revolvers in self-defense. These Yuraks are the nomadic portion of the Turkish peasantry. They live in caves or rudely constructed huts, shifting their habitation at will, or upon the exhaus-

AN ANGORA SHEPHERD.

tion of the pasturage. Their costume is most primitive both in style and material; the trousers and caps being made of sheepskin and the tunic of plaited wheat-straw. In contradistinction to the Yuraks the settled inhabitants of the country are called Turks. That term, however, which means rustic or clown, is never used by the Turks themselves except in derision or disdain; they always speak of themselves as " Osmanli."

The great length of the Angora fleece, which sometimes reaches eight inches, is due solely to the peculiar climate of the locality. The same goats taken elsewhere have not thriven. Even the Angora dogs and cats are remarkable for the extraordinary length of their fleecy covering. On nearing Angora itself, we raced at high speed over the undulating plateau. Our zaptieh on his jaded horse faded away in the dim distance, and we saw him no more. This was our last guard for many weeks to come, as we decided to dispense with an escort that really retarded us. But on reaching Erzerum, the Vali refused us permission to enter the district of Alashgerd without a guard, so we were forced to take one.

We were now on historic ground. To our right, on the Owas, a tributary of the Sakaria, was the little village of Istanas, where stood the ancient seat of Midas, the Phrygian king, and where Alexander the Great cut with his sword the Gordian knot to prove his right to the rulership of the world. On the plain, over which we were now skimming, the great Tatar, Timur, fought the memorable battle with Bajazet I., which resulted in the capture of the Ottoman conqueror. Since the time that the title of Asia applied to the small coast-province of Lydia, this country has been the theater for the grandest events in human history.

The old mud-houses of modern Angora, as we rolled

1, THE ENGLISH CONSUL AT ANGORA, FEEDING HIS PETS; 2, PASSING A CARAVAN OF CAMELS; 3, PLOWING IN ASIA MINOR.

into the city, contrasted strongly with the cyclopean walls of its ancient fortress. After two days in Angora we diverged from the direct route to Sivas through Yüzgat, so as to visit the city of Kaisarieh. Through the efforts of the progressive Vali at Angora, a macadamized road was in the course of construction to this point, a part of which—to the town of Kirshehr—was already completed. Although surrounded by unusual fertility and luxuriance for an interior town, the low mud-houses

A CONTRAST.

and treeless streets give Kirshehr that same thirsty and painfully uniform appearance which characterizes every village or city in Asiatic Turkey. The mud buildings of Babylon, and not the marble edifices of Nineveh, have served as models for the Turkish architect. We have seen the Turks, when making the mud-straw bricks used in house-building, scratch dirt for the purpose from between the marble slabs and boulders that lay in profusion over the ground. A few of the government buildings and some of the larger private residences are improved by a coat of whitewash, and now and then the warm spring showers bring out on the mud roofs a relieving verdure, that frequently serves as pasture for the family goat. Everything is low and contracted, especially the doorways. When a foreigner bumps his head, and demands the reason for such stupid architecture, he is met with that decisive answer, "Adet"— custom, the most powerful of all influences in Turkey and the East.

Our entry into Kirshehr was typical of our reception everywhere. When we were seen approaching, several horsemen came out to get a first look at our strange horses. They challenged us to a race, and set a spanking pace down into the streets of the town. Before we reached the *khan*, or inn, we were obliged to dismount. "Bin! bin!" ("Ride! ride!") went up in a shout. "Nimkin deyil" ("It is impossible"), we explained, in such a jam; and the crowd opened up three or four feet ahead of us. "Bin bocale" ("Ride, so that we can see"), they shouted again; and some of them rushed up to hold our steeds for us to mount. With the greatest difficulty we impressed upon our persistent assistants that they could not help us. By the time we reached the khan the crowd had become almost a mob, pushing and tumbling over one another, and yelling to every one in sight that "the devil's carts have come." The inn-keeper came out, and we had to assure him that the mob was actuated only by curiosity. As soon as the bicycles were over the threshold, the doors were bolted

A TURKISH FLOUR-MILL.

and braced. The crowds swarmed to the windows. While the khanji prepared coffee we sat down to watch the amusing by-play and repartee going on around us. Those who by virtue of their friendship with the khanji were admitted to the room with us began a tirade against the boyish curiosity of their less fortunate brethren on the outside. Their own curiosity assumed tangible shape. Our clothing, and even our hair and faces, were critically examined. When we attempted to jot down the day's events in our note-books they crowded closer than ever. Our fountain-pen was an additional puzzle to them. It was passed around, and explained and commented on at length.

Our camera was a "mysterious" black box. Some said it was a telescope, about which they had only a vague idea; others, that it was a box containing our money. But our map of Asiatic Turkey was to them the most curious thing of all. They spread it on the floor, and hovered over it, while we pointed to the towns and cities. How could we tell where the places were until we had been there? How did we even know their names? It was wonderful—wonderful! We traced for them our own journey, where we had been and where we were going, and then endeavored to show them how, by starting from our homes and continuing always in an easterly direction, we could at last reach our starting-point from the west. The more intelligent of them grasped the idea. "Around the world," they repeated again and again, with a mystified expression.

Relief came at last, in the person of a messenger from Osman Beg, the inspector-general of agriculture of the Angora vilayet, bearing an invitation to supper. He stated that he had already heard of our undertaking through the Constantinople press, and desired to make our acquaintance. His note, which was written in French, showed him to be a man of European education; and on shaking hands with him a half-hour later, we found him to be a man of European origin — an Albanian Greek, and a cousin of the Vali at Angora. He said a report had gone out that two devils were passing through the country. The dinner was one of those incongruous Turkish mixtures of sweet and sour, which was by no means relieved by the harrowing Turkish music which our host ground out from an antiquated hand-organ.

Although it was late when we returned to the khan, we found everybody still up. The room in which we were to sleep (there was only one room) was filled with a crowd of loiterers, and tobacco smoke. Some were playing games similar to our chess and backgammon, while others were looking on, and smoking the gurgling narghile, or water-pipe. The bicycles had been put away under lock and key, and the crowd gradually dispersed. We lay down in our

MILL IN ASIA MINOR.

GIPSIES OF ASIA MINOR.

clothes, and tried to lose consciousness; but the Turkish supper, the tobacco smoke, and the noise of the quarreling gamesters, put sleep out of the question. At midnight the sudden boom of a cannon reminded us that we were in the midst of the Turkish Ramadan. The sound of tramping feet, the beating of a bass drum, and the whining tones of a Turkish bagpipe, came over the midnight air. Nearer it came, and louder grew the sound, till it reached the inn door, where it remained for some time. The fast of Ramadan commemorates the revelation of the Koran to the prophet Mohammed. It lasts through the four phases of the moon. From daylight, or, as the Koran reads, "from the time you can distinguish a white thread from a black one," no good Mussulman will eat, drink, or smoke. At midnight the mosques are illuminated, and bands of music go about the streets all night, making a tremendous uproar. One cannon is fired at dusk, to announce the time to break the fast by eating supper, another at midnight to arouse the people for the preparation of breakfast, and still another at daylight as a signal for resuming the fast. This, of course, is very hard on the poor man who has to work during the day. As a precaution against oversleeping, a watchman goes about just before daybreak, and makes a rousing clatter at the gate of every Mussulman's house to warn him that if he wants anything to eat he must get it instanter. Our roommates evidently intended to make an "all night" of it, for they forthwith commenced the preparation of their morning meal. How it was despatched we do not know, for we fell asleep, and were only awakened by the muezzin on a neighboring minaret, calling to morning prayer.

Our morning ablutions were usually made *à la* Turk: by having water poured upon the hands from a spouted vessel. Cleanliness is, with the Turk, perhaps, more than ourselves, the next thing to godliness. But his ideas are based upon a very different theory. Although he uses no soap for washing either his person or his clothes, yet he considers himself much cleaner than the giaour, for the reason that he uses running water exclusively, never allowing the same particles to touch him the second time. A Turk believes that all water is purified after running six feet. As a test of his faith we have often seen him lading up drinking-water from a stream where the women were washing clothes just a few yards above.

As all cooking and eating had stopped at the sound of the morning cannon, we found great difficulty in gathering together even a cold breakfast of *ekmek, yaourt,* and raisins. Ekmek is a cooked bran-flour paste, which has the thinness, consistency, and almost the taste of blotting-paper. This is the Turkish peasant's staff of life. He carries it with him everywhere; so did we. As it was made in huge circular sheets, we would often punch a hole in the middle, and slip it up over our arms. This we found the handiest and most serviceable mode of transportation, being handy to eat without removing our hands from the handle-bars, and also answering the purpose of sails in case of a favoring wind. Yaourt, another almost universal food, is milk curdled with rennet. This, as well as all foods that are not liquid, they scoop up with a roll of ekmek, a part of the scoop being taken with every mouthful. Raisins here, as well as in many other parts of the country, are very cheap. We paid two piasters (about nine cents) for an *oche* (two and a half pounds), but we soon made the discovery that a Turkish oche contained a great many "stones"— which of course was purely accidental. Eggs, also, we found exceedingly cheap. On one occasion, twenty-five were set before us, in response to our call for eggs to the value of one piaster

SCENE AT A GREEK INN.

—four and a half cents. In Asiatic Turkey we had some extraordinary dishes served to us, including daintily prepared leeches. But the worst mixture, perhaps, was the "Bairam soup," which contains over a dozen ingredients, including peas, prunes, walnuts, cherries, dates, white and black beans, apricots, cracked wheat, raisins, etc.—all

EATING KAISERICHEN (EKMEK) OR BREAD.

mixed in cold water. Bairam is the period of feasting after the Ramadan fast.

On preparing to leave Kirshehr after our frugal breakfast we found that Turkish curiosity had extended even to the contents of our baggage, which fitted in the frames of the machines. There was nothing missing, however:

and we did not lose so much as a button during our sojourn among them. Thieving is not one of their faults, but they take much latitude in helping themselves. Many a time an inn-keeper would "help us out" by disposing of one third of a chicken that we had paid him a high price to prepare.

When we were ready to start the chief of police cleared a riding space through the streets, which for an hour had

GRINDING WHEAT.

been filled with people. As we passed among them they shouted "Oorooglar olsun" ("May good fortune attend you"). "Inshallah" ("If it please God"), we replied, and waved our helmets in acknowledgment.

At the village of Topakle, on the following night, our reception was not so innocent and good-natured. It was already dusk when we reached the outskirts of the village, where we were at once spied by a young man who was driving in the lowing herd. The alarm was given, and the people swarmed like so many rats from a corn-bin. We could see from their costume and features that they were not pure-blooded Turks. We asked if we could get food and lodging, to which they replied, "Evet, evet" ("Yes, yes"), but when we asked them where, they simply pointed ahead, and shouted, "Bin, bin!" We did not "bin" this time, because it was too dark, and the streets were bad. We walked, or rather were pushed along by the impatient rabble, and almost deafened by their shouts of "Bin, bin!" At the end of the village we repeated our question of where. Again they pointed ahead, and shouted, "Bin!" Finally an old man led us to what seemed to be a private residence, where we had to drag our bicycles up a dark narrow stairway to the second story. The crowd soon filled the room to suffocation, and were not disposed to heed our request to be left alone. One stalwart youth showed such a spirit of opposition that we were obliged to eject him upon a crowded stairway, causing the mob to go down like a row of tenpins. Then the owner of the house came in, and in an agitated manner declared he could not allow us to remain in his house overnight. Our reappearance caused a jeering shout to go up from the crowd; but no violence was attempted beyond the catching hold of the rear wheel

A TURKISH (HAMAAL) OR CARRIER.

when our backs were turned, and the throwing of clods of earth. They followed us, *en masse*, to the edge of the village, and there stopped short, to watch us till we disappeared in the darkness. The nights at this high altitude were chilly. We had no blankets, and not enough clothing to warrant a camp among the rocks. There was not a twig on the whole plateau with which to build a fire. We were alone, however, and that was rest in itself. After walking an hour, perhaps, we saw a light gleaming from a group of mudhuts a short distance off the road. From the numerous flocks around it, we took it to be a shepherds' village. Everything was quiet except the restless sheep, whose silky fleece glistened in the light of the rising moon.

TURKISH WOMEN GOING TO PRAYERS IN KAISARIEH.

Supper was not yet over, for we caught a whiff of its savory odor. Leaving our wheels outside, we entered the first door we came to, and, following along a narrow passageway, emerged into a room where four rather rough-looking shepherds were ladling the soup from a huge bowl in their midst. Before they were aware of our presence, we uttered the usual salutation "Sabala khayr olsun." This startled some little boys who were playing in the corner, who yelled, and ran into the haremlük, or women's apartment. This brought to the door the female occupants, who also uttered a shriek, and sunk back as if in a swoon. It was evident that the visits of giaours to this place had been few and far between. The shepherds returned our salutation with some hesitation, while their ladles dropped into the soup, and their gaze became fixed on our huge helmets, our dogskin top-coats, and abbreviated nether garments. The women by this time had sufficiently recovered from their nervous shock to give scope to their usual curiosity through the cracks in the partition. Confidence now being inspired by our own composure, we were invited to sit down and participate in the evening meal. Although it was only a gruel of sour milk and rice, we managed to make a meal off it. Meantime the wheels had been discovered by some passing neighbor. The news was spread throughout the village, and soon an excited throng came in with our bicycles borne upon the shoulders of two powerful Turks. Again we were besieged with entreaties to ride, and, hoping that this would gain for us a comfortable night's rest, we yielded, and, amid peals of laughter from a crowd of Turkish peasants, gave an exhibition in the moonlight. Our only reward, when we returned to our quarters, was two greasy pillows and a filthy carpet for a coverlet. But the much needed rest we did not secure, for the suspicions aroused by the first glance at our bed-cover proved to be well grounded.

About noon on April 20, our road turned abruptly into the broad caravan trail that runs between Smyrna and Kaisarieh, about ten miles west of the latter city. A long caravan of camels was moving majestically up the road, headed by a little donkey, which the *devedejee* (camel-driver) was riding with his feet dangling almost to the ground. That proverbially stubborn creature moved not a muscle until we came alongside, when all at once he gave one of his characteristic side lurches, and precipitated the rider to the ground. The first camel, with a protesting grunt, began to sidle off, and the broadside movement continued down the line till the whole caravan stood at an angle of

THE "FLIRTING TOWER" IN SIVAS.

about forty-five degrees to the road. The camel of Asia Minor does not share that antipathy for the equine species which is so general among their Asiatic cousins; but steel horses were more than even they could endure.

A sudden turn in the road now brought us in sight of old Arjish Dagh, which towers 13,000 feet above the city of Kaisarieh, and whose head and shoulders were covered with snow. Native tradition tells us that against this lofty summit the ark of Noah struck in the rising flood;

and for this reason Noah cursed it, and prayed that it might ever be covered with snow. It was in connection with this very mountain that we first conceived the idea of making the ascent of Ararat. Here and there, on some of the most prominent peaks, we could distinguish little

HOUSE OF THE AMERICAN CONSUL IN SIVAS.

mounds of earth, the ruined watch-towers of the prehistoric Hittites.

Kaisarieh (ancient Cæsarea) is filled with the ruins and the monuments of the fourteenth-century Seljuks. Arrowheads and other relics are every day unearthed there, to serve as toys for the street urchins. Since the development of steam-communication around the coast, it is no longer the caravan center that it used to be; but even now its *charshi*, or inclosed bazaars, are among the finest in Turkey, being far superior in appearance to those of Constantinople. These *charshi* are nothing more than narrow streets, inclosed by brick arches, and lined on either side with booths. It was through one of these that our only route to the khan lay — and yet we felt that in such contracted quarters, and in such an excited mob as had gathered around us, disaster was sure to follow. Our only salvation was to keep ahead of the jam, and get through as soon as possible. We started on the spurt; and the race began. The unsuspecting merchants and their customers were suddenly distracted from their thoughts of gain as we whirled by; the crowd close behind sweeping everything before it. The falling of barrels and boxes, the rattling of tin cans, the crashing of crockery, the howling of the vagrant dogs that were trampled under foot, only added to the general tumult.

Through the courtesy of Mr. Peet of the American Bible House at Constantinople, we were provided with letters of introduction to the missionaries at Kaisarieh, as well as elsewhere along our route through Asiatic Turkey, and upon them we also had drafts to the amount of our deposit made at the Bible House before starting. Besides, we owed much to the hospitality and kindness of these people. The most striking feature of the missionary work at Kaisarieh is the education of the Armenian women, whose social position seems to be even more degraded than that of their Turkish sisters. With the native Armenians, as with the Turks, fleshiness adds much to the price of a wife. The wife of a missionary is to them an object both of wonderment and contempt. As she walks along the street, they will whisper to one another: "There goes a woman who knows all her husband's business; and who can manage just as well as himself." This will generally be followed in an undertone by the expression, "Madana satana," which means, in common parlance, "a female devil." At first it was a struggle to overcome this ignorant prejudice, and to get girls to come to the school free of charge; now it is hard to find room for them even when they are asked to pay for their tuition.

The costume of the Armenian woman is generally of some bright-colored cloth, prettily trimmed. Her coiffure, always elaborate, sometimes includes a string of gold coins, encircling the head, or strung down the plait. A silver belt incloses the waist, and a necklace of coins calls attention to her pretty neck. When washing clothes by the stream, they frequently show a gold ring encircling an ankle.

In the simplicity of their costumes, as well as in the fact that they do not expose the face, the Turkish women stand in strong contrast to the Armenian. Baggy trousers *à la* Bloomer, a loose robe skirt opening at the sides, and a voluminous shawl-like girdle around the waist and body, constitute the main features of the Turkish indoor costume. On the street a shroud-like robe called yashmak, usually white, but sometimes crimson, purple, or black, covers them from head to foot. When we would meet a bevy of these creatures on the road in the dusk of evening, their white, fluttering garments would give them the appearance of winged celestials. The Turkish women are generally timorous of men, and especially so of foreigners. Those of the rural districts, however, are not so shy as their city cousins. We frequently met them at work in groups about the villages or in the open fields, and would sometimes ask for a drink of water. If they were a party of maidens, as was often the case, they would draw back and hide behind one another. We would offer one of them a ride on our "very nice horses." This would cause a general giggle among her companions, and a drawing of the yashmak closer about the neck and face.

The road scenes in the interior provinces are but little varied. One of the most characteristic features of the Anatolian landscape are the storks, which come in flocks of thousands from their winter quarters in Egypt and

ARABS CONVERSING WITH A TURK.

build summer nests, unmolested, on the village housetops. These, like the crows, magpies, and swallows, prove valuable allies to the husbandmen in their war against the locust. A still more serviceable friend in this direction is the *smarmar*, a pink thrush with black wings. Besides the various caravan trains of camels, donkeys, horses, and mules, the road is frequently dotted with ox-carts, run on solid wooden wheels without tires, and drawn by that peculiar bovine species, the buffalo. With their distended necks, elevated snouts, and hog-like bristles, these animals present an ugly appearance, especially when wallowing in mud puddles.

Now and then in the villages we passed by a primitive flour-mill moved by a small stream playing upon a horizontal wheel beneath the floor; or, more primitive still, by a blindfolded donkey plodding ceaselessly around in his circular path. In the streets we frequently encountered boys and old men gathering manure for their winter fuel; and now and then a cripple or invalid would accost us as "Hakim" ("Doctor"), for the medical work of the missionaries has given these simple-minded folk the impression that all foreigners are physicians. Coming up and extending a hand for us to feel the pulse they would ask us to do something for the disease, which we could see was rapidly carrying them to the grave.

Our first view of Sivas was obtained from the top of Mount Yildiz, on which still stands the ruined castle of Mithridates, the Pontine monarch, whom Lucullus many times defeated, but never conquered. From this point we made a very rapid descent, crossed the Kizil Irmak for the third time by an old ruined bridge, and half an hour later saw the "stars and stripes" flying above the U. S. consulate. In the society of our representative, Mr. Henry M. Jewett, we were destined to spend several weeks; for a day or two after our arrival, one

A KADI EXPOUNDING THE KORAN.

of us was taken with a slight attack of typhoid fever, supposed to have been contracted by drinking from the roadside streams. No better place could have been chosen for such a mishap; for recovery was speedy in such comfortable quarters, under the care of the missionary ladies.

The comparative size and prosperity of Sivas, in the midst of rather barren surroundings, are explained by the fact that it lies at the converging point of the chief caravan routes between the Euxine, Euphrates, and Mediterranean. Besides being the capital of Rumili, the former Seljuk province of Cappadocia, it is the place of residence for a French and American consular representative, and an agent of the Russian government for the collection of the war indemnity, stipulated in the treaty of '78. The dignity of office is here upheld with something of the pomp and splendor of the East, even by the representative of democratic America. In our tours with Mr. Jewett we were escorted at the head by a Circassian *cavass* (Turkish police), clothed in a long black coat, with a huge dagger dangling from a belt of cartridges. Another native cavass, with a broadsword dragging at his side, usually brought up the rear. At night he was the one to carry the huge lantern, which, according to the number of candles, is the insignia of rank. "I must give the Turks what they want," said the consul, with a twinkle in his eye — "form and red tape. I would not be a consul in their eyes, if I didn't." To illustrate the formality of Turkish etiquette he told this story: "A Turk was once engaged in saving furniture from his burning home, when he noticed that a bystander was rolling a cigarette. He immediately stopped in his hurry, struck a match, and offered a light."

The most flagrant example of Turkish formality that

EVENING HALT IN A VILLAGE.

came to our notice was the following address on an official document to the Sultan:

"The Arbiter; the Absolute; the Soul and Body of the Universe; the Father of all the sovereigns of the earth; His Excellency, the Eagle Monarch; the Cause of the never-changing order of things; the Source of all honor; the Son of the Sultan of Sultans, under whose feet we are dust, whose awful shadow protects us; Abdul Hamid II., Son of Abdul Medjid, whose residence is in Paradise; our glorious Lord, to whose sacred body be given health, and strength, and endless days; whom Allah keeps in his palace, and on his throne with joy and glory, forever. Amen."

PRIMITIVE WEAVING.

This is not the flattery of a cringing subordinate, for the same spirit is revealed in an address by the Sultan himself to his Grand Vizir:

"Most honored Vizir; Maintainer of the good order of the World; Director of public affairs with wisdom and judgment; Accomplisher of the important transactions of mankind with intelligence and good sense; Consolidator of the edifice of Empire and of Glory; endowed by the Most High with abundant gifts; and 'Moushir,' at this time, of my Gate of Felicity; my Vizir Mehmed Pasha, may God be pleased to preserve him long in exalted dignity."

Though the Turks cannot be called lazy, yet they like to take their time. Patience, they say, belongs to God; hurry, to the devil. Nowhere is this so well illustrated as in the manner of shopping in Turkey. This was brought particularly to our notice when we visited the Sivas bazaars to examine some inlaid silverware, for which the place is celebrated. The customer stands in the street inspecting the articles on exhibition; the merchant sits on his heels on the booth floor. If the customer is of some position in life, he climbs up and sits down on a level with the merchant. If he is a foreigner, the merchant is quite deferential. A merchant is not a merchant at all, but a host entertaining a guest. Coffee is served; then a cigarette rolled up and handed to the "guest," while the various social and other local topics are freely discussed. After coffee and smoking the question of purchase is gradually approached; not abruptly, as that would involve a loss of dignity; but circumspectly, as if the buying of anything were a mere afterthought. Maybe, after half an hour, the customer has indicated what he wants, and after discussing the quality of the goods, the customer asks the price in an off-hand way, as though he were not particularly interested. The merchant replies, "Oh, whatever your highness pleases," or, "I shall be proud if your highness will do me the honor to accept it as a gift." This means nothing whatever, and is merely the introduction to the haggling which is sure to follow. The seller, with silken manners and brazen countenance, will always name a price four times as large as it should be. Then the real business begins. The buyer offers one half or one fourth of what he finally expects to pay; and a war of words, in a blustering tone, leads up to the close of this every-day farce.

The superstition of the Turks is nowhere so apparent as in their fear of the "evil eye." Jugs placed around the edge of the roof, or an old shoe filled with garlic and blue beets (blue glass balls or rings) are a sure guard against this illusion. Whenever a pretty child is playing upon the street the passers-by will say: "Oh, what an ugly child!" for fear of inciting the evil spirit against its beauty. The peasant classes in Turkey are of course the most superstitious because they are the most ignorant. They have no education whatever, and can neither read nor write. Stamboul is the only great city of which they know. Paris is a term signifying the whole outside world. An American missionary was once asked: "In what part of Paris is America?" Yet it can be said that they are generally honest, and always patient. They earn from about six to eight cents a day. This will furnish them with ekmek and pilaff, and that is all they expect. They eat meat only on feast-days, and then only mutton. The tax-gatherer is their only grievance; they look upon him as a necessary evil. They have no idea of being ground down under the oppressor's iron heel. Yet they are happy because they are contented, and have no envy. The poorer, the more ignorant, a Turk is, the better he seems to be. As he gets money and power, and becomes "contaminated" by western civilization, he deteriorates. A resident of twenty years' experience said: "In the lowest classes I have sometimes found truth, honesty, and gratitude; in the middle classes, seldom; in the highest, never." The corruptibility of the Turkish official is almost proverbial; but such is to be expected in the land where "the public treasury" is regarded as a "sea," and "who does not drink of it, as a pig." Peculation and malversation are fully expected in the public official. They are necessary evils—*adet* (custom) has made them so. Offices are sold to the highest bidder. The Turkish official is one of the politest and most agreeable of men. He is profuse in his compliments, but he has no conscience as to bribes, and little regard for virtue as its own reward. We are glad to be able to record a brilliant, though perhaps theoretical, exception to this general rule. At Koch-Hissar, on our way from Sivas to Kara Hissar, a delay was caused by a rather serious break in one of our bicycles. In the interval we were the invited guests of a district kadi, a venerable-looking and genial old gentleman whose acquaintance we had made in an official visit on the previous day, as he was then the acting *caimacam* (mayor). His house was situated in a neighboring valley in the shadow of a towering bluff. We were ushered into the *selamlük*, or guest apartment, in company with an Armenian friend who had been educated as a doctor in America, and who had consented to act as interpreter for the occasion.

The kadi entered with a smile on his countenance, and made the usual picturesque form of salutation by describing the figure 3 with his right hand from the floor to his forehead. Perhaps it was because he wanted to be polite that he said he had enjoyed our company on the previous day, and had determined, if possible, to have a more extended conversation. With the usual coffee and cigarettes, the kadi became informal and chatty. He was evidently a firm believer in predestination, as he remarked that God had foreordained our trip to that country, even the food we were to eat, and the invention of the extraordinary "cart" on which we were to ride. The idea of such a journey, in such a peculiar way, was not to be accredited to the ingenuity of man. There was a purpose in it all. When we ventured to thank him for his hospitality toward two strangers, and even foreigners, he said that this world occupied so small a space in God's dominion, that we could well afford to be brothers, one to another, in spite of our individual beliefs and opinions. "We may have different religious beliefs," said he, "but we all belong to the same great father of humanity; just as children of different complexions, dispositions, and intellects may belong to one common parent. We should exercise reason always, and have charity for other people's opinions."

From charity the conversation naturally turned to justice. We were much interested in his opinion on this subject, as that of a Turkish judge, and rather high official. "Justice," said he, "should be administered to the humblest person; though a king should be the offending party, all alike must yield to the sacred law of justice. We must account to God for our acts, and not to men."

The regular route from Sivas to Erzerum passes through Erzinjan. From this, however, we diverged at Zara, in order to visit the city of Kara Hissar, and the neighboring Lidjissy mines, which had been pioneered by the Genoese explorers, and were now being worked by a party of Englishmen. This divergence on to unbeaten paths was made at a very inopportune season; for the rainy spell set in, which lasted, with scarcely any intermission, for over a fortnight. At the base of Kosse Dagh, which stands upon the watershed between the two largest rivers of Asia Minor, the Kizil Irmak and Yeshil Irmak, our road was blocked by a mountain freshet, which at its height washed everything before it. We spent a day and night on its bank, in a primitive flour-mill, which was so far removed from domestic life that we had to send three miles up in the mountains to get something to eat. The Yeshil Irmak, which we crossed just before reaching Kara

Hissar, was above our shoulders as we waded through, holding our bicycles and baggage over our heads; while the swift current rolled the small boulders against us, and almost knocked us off our feet. There were no bridges in this part of the country. With horses and wagons the rivers were usually fordable; and what more would you want? With the Turk, as with all Asiatics, it is not a question of what is better, but what will do. Long before we reached a stream, the inhabitants of a certain town

A FERRY IN ASIA MINOR.

or village would gather round, and with troubled countenances say, "Christian gentlemen — there is no bridge," pointing to the river beyond, and graphically describing that it was over our horses' heads. That would settle it, they thought; it never occurred to them that a "Christian gentleman" could take off his clothes and wade. Sometimes, as we walked along in the mud, the wheels of our bicycles would become so clogged that we could not even push them before us. In such a case we would take the nearest shelter, whatever it might be. The night before reaching Kara Hissar, we entered an abandoned stable, from which everything had fled except the fleas. Another night was spent in the pine-forests just on the border between Asia Minor and Armenia, which were said to be the haunts of the border robbers. Our surroundings could not be relieved by a fire for fear of attracting their attention.

When at last we reached the Trebizond-Erzerum highway at Baiboot, the contrast was so great that the scaling of Kop Dagh, on its comparatively smooth surface, was a mere breakfast spell. From here we looked down for the first time into the valley of the historic Euphrates, and a few hours later we were skimming over its bottom lands toward the embattled heights of Erzerum.

As we neared the city, some Turkish peasants in the fields caught sight of us, and shouted to their companions: "Russians! Russians! There they are! Two of them!" This was not the first time we had been taken for the subjects of the Czar; the whole country seemed to be in dread of them. Erzerum is the capital of that district which Russia will no doubt demand, if the stipulated war indemnity is not paid.

The entrance into the city was made to twist and turn among the ramparts, so as to avoid a rush in case of an attack. But this was no proof against a surprise in the case of the noiseless wheel. In we dashed with a roaring wind, past the affrighted guards, and were fifty yards away before they could collect their scattered senses. Then suddenly it dawned upon them that we were human beings, and foreigners besides—perhaps even the dreaded Russian spies. They took after us at full speed, but it was too late. Before they reached us we were in the house of the commandant pasha, the military governor, to whom we had a letter of introduction from our consul at Sivas. That gentleman we found extremely good-natured; he laughed heartily at our escapade with the guards. Nothing would do but we must visit the Vali, the civil governor, who was also a pasha of considerable reputation and influence.

We had intended, but not so soon, to pay an official visit to the Vali to present our letter from the Grand Vizir, and to ask his permission to proceed to Bayazid, whence we had planned to attempt the ascent of Mount

A VILLAGE SCENE.

Ararat, an experience which will be described in the next chapter. A few days before, we heard, a similar application had been made by an English traveler from Bagdad, but owing to certain suspicions the permission was refused. It was with no little concern, therefore, that we approached the Vali's private office in company with his

French interpreter. Circumstances augured ill at the very start. The Vali was evidently in a bad humor, for we overheard him storming in a high key at some one in the room with him. As we passed under the heavy matted curtains the two attendants who were holding them up cast a rather horrified glance at our dusty shoes and unconventional costume. The Vali was sitting in a large arm-chair in front of a very small desk, placed at the far end of a vacant-looking room. After the usual salaams, he motioned to a seat on the divan, and proceeded at once to examine our credentials while we sipped at our coffee, and whiffed the small cigarettes which were immediately served. This furnished the Vali an opportunity to regain his usual composure. He was evidently an autocrat of the severest type; if we pleased him, it would be all right; if we did not, it would be all wrong. We showed him everything we had, from our Chinese passport to the little photographic camera, and related some of the most amusing incidents of our journey through his country. From the numerous questions he asked we felt certain of his genuine interest, and were more than pleased to see an occasional broad smile on his countenance. "Well," said he, as we rose to take leave, "your passports will be ready any time after to-morrow; in the mean time I shall be pleased to have your horses quartered and fed at government expense." This was a big joke for a Turk, and assured us of his good-will.

A bicycle exhibition which the Vali had requested was given the morning of our departure for Bayazid, on a level stretch of road just outside the city. Several missionaries and members of the consulates had gone out in carriages, and formed a little group by themselves. We rode up with the "stars and stripes" and "star and crescent" fluttering side by side from the handle-bars. It was always our custom, especially on diplomatic occasions, to have a little flag of the country associated with that of our own. This little arrangement evoked a smile from the Vali, who, when the exhibition was finished, stepped forward and said, "I am satisfied, I am pleased." His richly caparisoned white charger was now brought up. Leaping into the saddle, he waved us good-by, and moved away with his suite toward the city. We ourselves remained for a few moments to bid good-by to our hospitable friends, and then, once more, continued our journey toward the east.

II

THE ASCENT OF MOUNT ARARAT

ACCORDING to tradition, Mount Ararat is the scene of two of the most important events in the history of the human race. In the sacred land of Eden, which Armenian legend places at its base, the first of human life was born; and on its solitary peak the last of human life was saved from an all-destroying flood. The remarkable geographical position of this mountain seems to justify the Armenian view that it is the center of the world. It is on the longest line drawn through the Old World from the Cape of Good Hope to Bering Strait; it is also on the line of the great deserts and inland seas stretching from Gibraltar to Lake Baikal in Siberia—a line of continuous depressions; it is equidistant from the Black and Caspian Seas and the Mesopotamian plain, which three depressions are now watered by three distinct river-systems emanating from Ararat's immediate vicinity. No other region has seen or heard so much of the story of mankind. In its grim presence empires have come and gone; cities have risen and fallen; human life has soared up on the wings of hope, and dashed against the rocks of despair.

To the eye Ararat presents a gently inclined slope of

sand and ashes rising into a belt of green, another zone of black volcanic rocks streaked with snow-beds, and then a glittering crest of silver. From the burning desert at its base to the icy pinnacle above, it rises through a vertical distance of 13,000 feet. There are but few peaks in the world that rise so high (17,250 feet above sea-level) from so low a plain (2000 feet on the Russian, and 4000 feet on the Turkish, side), and which, therefore, present so grand a spectacle. Unlike many of the world's mountains, it stands alone. Little Ararat (12,840 feet above sea-level), and the other still smaller heights that dot the plain, only serve as a standard by which to measure Ararat's immensity and grandeur.

Little Ararat is the meeting-point, or corner-stone, of three great empires. On its conical peak converge the dominions of the Czar, the Sultan, and the Shah. The Russian border-line runs from Little Ararat along the high ridge which separates it from Great Ararat, through the peak of the latter, and onward a short distance to the northwest, then turns sharply to the west. On the Sardarbulakh pass, between Great and Little Ararat, is stationed a handful of Russian Cossacks to remind lawless tribes of the guardianship of the "White Sultan."

The two Ararats together form an elliptical mass, about twenty-five miles in length, running northwest and southeast, and about half that in width. Out of this massive base rise the two Ararat peaks, their bases being contiguous up to 8800 feet and their tops about seven miles apart. Little Ararat is an almost perfect truncated cone, while Great Ararat is more of a broad-shouldered dome supported by strong, rough-ribbed buttresses. The isolated position of Ararat, its structure of igneous rocks, the presence of small craters and immense volcanic fissures on its slopes, and the scoriæ and ashes on the surrounding plain, establish beyond a doubt its volcanic origin. But according to the upheaval theory of the eminent geologist, Hermann Abich, who was among the few to make the ascent of the mountain, there never was a great central crater in either Great or Little Ararat. Certain it is that no craters or signs of craters now exist on the summit of either mountain. But Mr. James Bryce, who made the last ascent, in 1876, seems to think that there is no sufficient reason why craters could not have previously existed, and been filled up by their own irruptions. There is no record of any irruption in historical times. The only thing approaching it was the earthquake which shook the mountain in 1840, accompanied by subterranean rumblings, and destructive blasts of wind. The Tatar village of Arghuri and a Kurdish encampment on the northeast slope were entirely destroyed by the precipitated rocks. Not a man was left to tell the story. Mr. Bryce and others have spoken of the astonishing height of the snow-line on Mount Ararat, which is placed at 14,000 feet; while in the Alps it is only about 9000 feet, and in the Caucasus on an average 11,000 feet, although they lie in a very little higher latitude. They assign, as a reason for this, the exceptionally dry region in which Ararat is situated. Mr. Bryce ascended the mountain on September 12, when the snow-line was at its very highest, the first large snow-bed he encountered being at 12,000 feet. Our own ascent being made as early as July 4,—in fact, the earliest ever recorded,—we found some snow as low as 8000 feet, and large beds at 10,500 feet. The top of Little Ararat was still at that time streaked with snow, but not covered. With so many extensive snow-beds, one would naturally expect to find copious brooks and streams flowing down the mountain into the plain; but owing to the porous and dry nature

of the soil, the water is entirely lost before reaching the base of the mountain. Even as early as July we saw no stream below 6000 feet, and even above this height the mountain freshets frequently flowed far beneath the surface under the loosely packed rocks, bidding defiance to our efforts to reach them. Notwithstanding the scarcity of snow-freshets, there is a middle zone on Mount Ararat, extending from about 5000 feet to 9000 feet elevation, which is covered with good pasturage, kept green by heavy dews and frequent showers. The hot air begins to rise from the desert plain as the morning sun peeps over the horizon, and continues through the day; this warm current, striking against the snow-covered summit, is condensed into clouds and moisture. In consequence, the top of Ararat is usually—during the summer months, at least—obscured by clouds from some time after dawn until sunset. On the last day of our ascent, however, we were particularly fortunate in having a clear summit until 1 : 15 in the afternoon.

Among the crags of the upper slope are found only a few specimens of the wild goat and sheep, and, lower down, the fox, wolf, and lynx. The bird and insect life is very scanty, but lizards and scorpions, especially on the lowest slopes, are abundant. The rich pasturage of Ararat's middle zone attracts pastoral Kurdish tribes. These nomadic shepherds, a few Tatars at New Arghuri, and a camp of Russian Cossacks at the well of Sardarbulakh, are the only human beings to disturb the quiet solitude of this grandest of nature's sanctuaries.

The first recorded ascent of Mount Ararat was in 1829, by Dr. Frederick Parrot, a Russo-German professor in the University of Dorpat. He reached the summit with a party of three Armenians and two Russian soldiers, after two unsuccessful attempts. His ascent, however, was doubted, not only by the people in the neighborhood, but by many men of science and position in the Russian empire, notwithstanding his clear account, which has been confirmed by subsequent observers, and in spite of the testimony of the two Russian soldiers who had gone with him.[1] Two of the Armenians who reached the summit with him declared that they had gone to a great height, but at the point where they had left off had seen much higher tops rising around them. This, thereupon, became the opinion of the whole country. After Antonomoff, in 1834, Herr Abich, the geologist, made his valuable ascent in 1845. He reached the eastern summit, which is only a few feet lower than the western, and only a few minutes' walk from it, but was obliged to return at once on account of the threatening weather. When he produced his companions as witnesses before the authorities at Erivan, they turned against him, and solemnly swore that at the point which they had reached a higher peak stood between them and the western horizon. This strengthened the Armenian belief in the inaccessibility of Ararat, which was not dissipated when the Russian military engineer, General Chodzko, and an English party made the ascent

[1] Eight years before the first recorded ascent of Ararat by Dr. Parrot (1829), there appeared the following from "Travels in Georgia, Persia, Armenia, and Ancient Babylonia," by Sir Robert Ker Porter, who, in his time, was an authority on southwestern Asia: "These inaccessible heights [of Mount Ararat] have never been trod by the foot of man since the days of Noah, if even then; for my idea is that the Ark rested in the space between the two heads (Great and Little Ararat), and not on the top of either. Various attempts have been made in different ages to ascend these tremendous mountain pyramids, but in vain. Their forms, snows, and glaciers are insurmountable obstacles: the distance being so great from the commencement of the icy region to the highest points, cold alone would be the destruction of any one who had the hardihood to persevere."

in 1856. Nor were their prejudiced minds convinced by the ascent of Mr. Bryce twenty years later, in 1876. Two days after his ascent, that gentleman paid a visit to the Armenian monastery at Echmiadzin, and was presented to the archimandrite as the Englishman who had just ascended to the top of "Masis." "No," said the ecclesiastical dignitary; "that cannot be. No one has ever been there. It is impossible." Mr. Bryce himself says: "I am persuaded that there is not a person living within sight of Ararat, unless it be some exceptionally educated Russian official at Erivan, who believes that any human foot, since Father Noah's, has trodden that sacred summit. So much stronger is faith than sight; or rather so much stronger is prejudice than evidence."

We had expected, on our arrival in Bayazid, to find in waiting for us a Mr. Richardson, an American missionary from Erzerum. Two years later, on our arrival home, we received a letter explaining that on his way from Van he had been captured by Kurdish brigands, and held a prisoner until released through the intervention of the British consul at Erzerum. It was some such fate as this that was predicted for us, should we ever attempt the ascent of Mount Ararat through the lawless Kurdish tribes upon its slopes. Our first duty, therefore, was to see the mutessarif of Bayazid, to whom we bore a letter from the Grand Vizir of Turkey, in order to ascertain what protection and assistance he would be willing to give us. We found with him a Circassian who belonged to the Russian camp at Sardarbulakh, on the Ararat pass, and who had accompanied General Chodzko on his ascent of the mountain in 1856. Both he and the mutessarif thought an ascent so early in the year was impossible; that we ought not to think of such a thing until two months later. It was now six weeks earlier than the time of General Chodzko's ascent (August 11 to 18), then the earliest on record. They both strongly recommended the northwestern slope as being more gradual. This is the one that Parrot ascended in 1829, and where Abich was repulsed on his third attempt. Though entirely inexperienced in mountain-climbing, we ourselves thought that the southeast slope, the one taken by General Chodzko, the English party, and Mr. Bryce, was far more feasible for a small party. One thing, however, the mutessarif was determined upon: we must not approach the mountain without an escort of Turkish zaptiehs, as an emblem of government protection. Besides, he would send for the chief of the Ararat Kurds, and endeavor to arrange with him for our safety and guidance up the mountain. As we emerged into the streets an Armenian professor gravely shook his head. "Ah," said he, "you will never do it." Then dropping his voice, he told us that those other ascents were all fictitious; that the summit of "Masis" had never yet been reached except by Noah; and that we were about to attempt what was an utter impossibility.

In Bayazid we could not procure even proper wood for alpenstocks. Willow branches, two inches thick, very dry and brittle, were the best we could obtain. Light as this wood is, the alpenstocks weighed at least seven pounds apiece when the iron hooks and points were riveted on at the ends by the native blacksmith, for whom we cut paper patterns, of the exact size, for everything we wanted. We next had large nails driven into the souls of our shoes by a local shoemaker, who made them for us by hand out of an old English file, and who wanted to pull them all out again because we would not pay him the exorbitant price he demanded. In buying provisions for the expedition, we spent three hours among the half dilapidated bazaars

WHERE THE "ZAPTIEHS" WERE NOT A NUISANCE.

of the town, which have never been repaired since the disastrous Russian bombardment. The most difficult task, perhaps, in our work of preparation was to strike a bargain with an Armenian muleteer to carry our food and baggage up the mountain on his two little donkeys.

Evening came, and no word from either the mutessarif or the Kurdish chief. Although we were extremely anxious to set off on the expedition before bad weather set in, we must not be in a hurry, for the military governor of Karakillissa was now the guest of the mutessarif, and it would be an interference with his social duties to try to see him until after his guest had departed. On the morrow we were sitting in our small dingy room after dinner, when a cavalcade hastened up to our inn, and a few minutes later we were surprised to hear ourselves addressed in our native tongue. Before us stood a dark-complexioned young man, and at his side a small wiry old gentleman, who proved to be a native Austrian Tyrolese, who followed the profession of an artist in Paris. He was now making his way to Erivan, in Russia, on a sight-seeing tour from Trebizond. His companion was a Greek from Salonica, who had lived for several years in London, whence he had departed not many weeks before, for Teheran, Persia. These two travelers had met in Constantinople, and the young Greek, who could speak English, Greek, and Turkish, had been acting as interpreter for the artist. They had heard of the "devil's carts" when in Van, and had made straight for our quarters on their arrival in Bayazid. At this point they were to separate. When we learned that the old gentleman (Ignaz Raffl by name) was a member of an Alpine club and an experienced mountain-climber, we urged him to join in the ascent. Though his shoulders were bent by the cares and troubles of sixty-three years, we finally induced him to accompany our party. Kantsa, the Greek, reluctantly agreed to do likewise, and proved to be an excellent interpreter, but a poor climber.

The following morning we paid the mutessarif a second visit, with Kantsa as interpreter. Inasmuch as the Kurdish chief had not arrived, the mutessarif said he would make us bearers of a letter to him. Two zaptiehs were to accompany us in the morning, while others were to go ahead and announce our approach.

At ten minutes of eleven, on the morning of the second of July, our small cavalcade, with the two exasperating donkeys at the head laden with mats, bags of provisions, extra clothing, alpenstocks, spiked shoes, and coils of stout rope, filed down the streets of Bayazid, followed by a curious rabble. As Bayazid lies hidden behind a projecting spur of the mountains we could obtain no view of the peak itself until we had tramped some distance out on the plain. Its huge giant mass broke upon us all at once. We stopped and looked—and looked again. No mountain-peak we have seen, though several have been higher, has ever inspired the feeling which filled us when we looked for the first time upon towering Ararat. We had not proceeded far before we descried a party of Kurdish horsemen approaching from the mountain. Our zaptiehs advanced rather cautiously to meet them, with rifles thrown across the pommels of their saddles. After a rather mysterious parley, our zaptiehs signaled that all was well. On coming up, they reported that these horsemen belonged to the party that was friendly to the Turkish government. The Kurds, they said, were at this time divided among themselves, a portion of them having adopted conciliatory measures with the government, and the rest holding aloof. But we rather considered their

READY FOR THE START.

little performance as a scheme to extort a little more baksheesh for their necessary presence.

The plain we were now on was drained by a tributary of the Aras River, a small stream reached after two hours' steady tramping. From the bordering hillocks we emerged in a short time upon another vast plateau, which stretched far away in a gentle rise to the base of the mountain itself. Near by we discovered a lone willow-tree, the only one in the whole sweep of our vision, under the gracious foliage of which sat a band of Kurds, retired from the heat of the afternoon sun, their horses feeding on some swamp grass near at hand. Attracted by this sign of water, we drew near, and found a copious spring. A few words from the zaptiehs, who had advanced among them, seemed to put the Kurds at their ease, though they did not by any means appease their curiosity. They invited us to partake of their frugal lunch of ekmek and goat's-milk cheese. Our clothes and baggage were discussed piece by piece, with loud expressions of merriment, until one of us arose, and, stealing behind the group, snapped the camera. "What was that?" said a burly member of the group, as he looked round with scowling face at his companions. "Yes; what was that?" they echoed, and then made a rush for the manipulator of the black box, which they evidently took for some instrument of the black art. The photographer stood serenely innocent, and winked at the zaptieh to give the proper explanation. He was equal to the occasion. "That," said he, "is an instrument for taking time by the sun." At this the box went the round, each one gazing intently into the lens, then scratching his head, and casting a bewildered look at his nearest neighbor. We noticed that every one about us was armed with knife, revolver, and Martini rifle, a belt of cartridges surrounding his waist. It occurred to us that Turkey was adopting a rather poor method of clipping the wings of these mountain birds, by selling them the very best equipments for war. Legally, none but government guards are permitted to carry arms, and yet both guns and ammunition are sold in the bazaars of almost every city of the Turkish dominions. The existence of these people, in their wild, semi-independent state, shows not so much the power of the Kurds as the weakness of the Turkish government, which desires to use a people of so fierce a reputation for the suppression of its other subjects. After half an hour's rest, we prepared to decamp, and so did our Kurdish companions. They were soon in their saddles, and galloping away in front of us, with their arms clanking, and glittering in the afternoon sunlight.

At the spring we had turned off the trail that led over the Sardarbulakh pass into Russia, and were now following a horse-path which winds up to the Kurdish encampments on the southern slope of the mountain. The plain was strewn with sand and rocks, with here and there a bunch of tough, wiry grass about a foot and a half high, which, though early in the year, was partly dry. It would have been hot work except for the rain of the day before and a strong southeast wind. As it was, our feet were blistered and bruised, the thin leather sandals worn at the outset offering very poor protection. The atmosphere being dry, though not excessively hot, we soon began to suffer from thirst. Although we searched diligently for water, we did not find it till after two hours more of constant marching, when at a height of about 6000 feet, fifty yards from the path, we discerned a picturesque cascade of sparkling, cold mountain water. Even the old gentleman, Raffl, joined heartily in the gaiety induced by this clear, cold water from Ararat's melting snows.

PARLEYING WITH THE KURDISH PARTY AT THE SPRING.

Our ascent for two and a half hours longer was through a luxuriant vegetation of flowers, grasses, and weeds, which grew more and more scanty as we advanced. Prominent among the specimens were the wild pink, poppy, and rose. One small fragrant herb, that was the most abundant of all, we were told was used by the Kurds for making tea. All these filled the evening air with perfume as we trudged along, passing now and then a Kurdish lad, with his flock of sheep and goats feeding on the mountain-grass, which was here much more luxuriant than below. Looking backward, we saw that we were higher than the precipitous cliffs which overtower the town of Bayazid, and which are perhaps from 1500 to 2000 feet above the lowest part of the plain. The view over the plateau was now grand. Though we were all fatigued by the day's work, the cool, moisture-laden air of evening revived our flagging spirits. We forged ahead with nimble step, joking, and singing a variety of national airs. The French "Marseillaise," in which the old gentleman heartily joined, echoed and reëchoed among the rocks, and caused the shepherd lads and their flocks to crane their heads in wonderment. Even the Armenian muleteer so far overcame his fear of the Kurdish robbers as to indulge in one of his accustomed funeral dirges; but it stopped short, never to go again, when we came in sight of the Kurdish encampment. The poor fellow instinctively grabbed his donkeys about their necks, as though they were about to plunge over a precipice. The zaptiehs dashed ahead with the mutessarif's letter to the Kurdish chief. We followed slowly on foot, while the Armenian and his two pets kept at a respectful distance in the rear.

The disk of the sun had already touched the western horizon when we came to the black tents of the Kurdish encampment, which at this time of the day presented a rather busy scene. The women seemed to be doing all the work, while their lords sat round on their haunches. Some of the women were engaged in milking the sheep and goats in an inclosure. Others were busy making butter in a churn which was nothing more than a skin vessel three feet long, of the shape of a Brazil-nut, suspended from a rude tripod; this they swung to and fro to the tune of a weird Kurdish song. Behind one of the tents, on a primitive weaving-machine, some of them were making tent-roofing and matting. Others still were walking about with a ball of wool in one hand and a distaff in the other, spinning yarn. The flocks stood round about, bleating and lowing, or chewing their cud in quiet contentment. All seemed very domestic and peaceful except the Kurdish dogs, which set upon us with loud, fierce growls and gnashing teeth.

Not so was it with the Kurdish chief, who by this time had finished reading the mutessarif's message, and who now advanced from his tent with salaams of welcome. As he stood before us in the glowing sunset, he was a rather tall, but well-proportioned man, with black eyes and dark mustache, contrasting well with his brown-tanned complexion. Upon his face was the stamp of a rather wild and retiring character, although treachery and deceit were by no means wanting. He wore a headgear that was something between a hat and a turban, and over his baggy Turkish trousers hung a long Persian coat of bright-colored, large-figured cloth, bound at the waist by a belt of cartridges. Across the shoulders was slung a breech-loading Martini rifle, and from his neck dangled a heavy gold chain, which was probably the spoil of some predatory expedition. A quiet dignity sat on Ismail Deverish's stalwart form.

It was with no little pleasure that we accepted his invi-

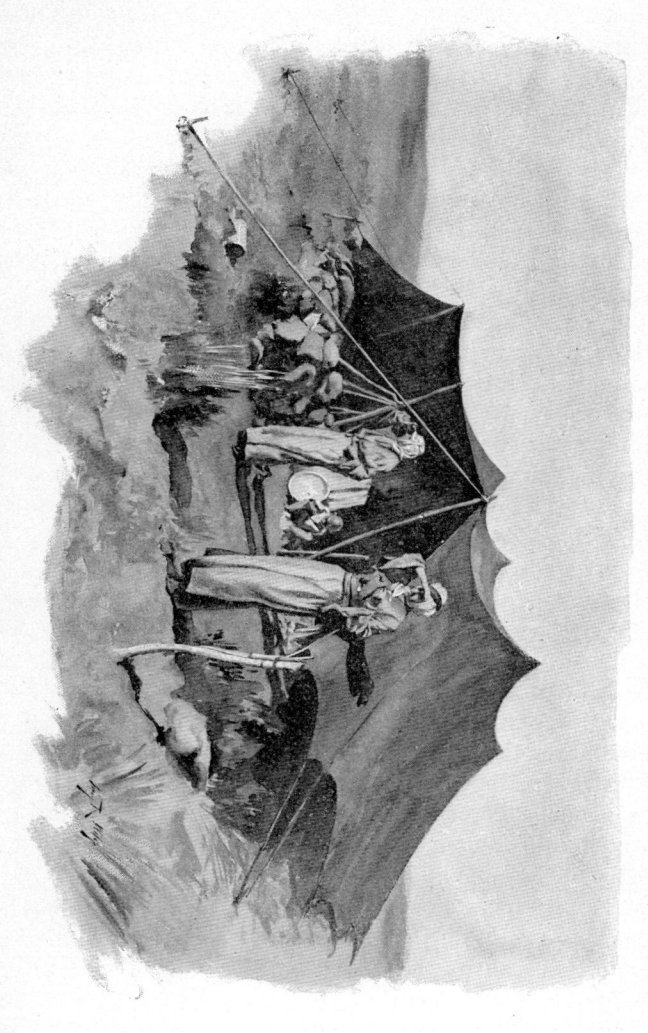

THE KURDISH ENCAMPMENT.

tation to a cup of tea. After our walk of nineteen miles, in which we had ascended from 3000 to 7000 feet, we were in fit condition to appreciate a rest. That Kurdish tent, as far as we were concerned, was a veritable palace, although we were almost blinded by the smoke from the green pine-branches on the smoldering fire. We said that the chief invited us to a cup of tea: so he did — but we provided the tea; and that, too, not only for our own party, but for half a dozen of the chief's personal friends. There being only two glasses in the camp, we of course had to wait until our Kurdish acquaintances had quenched their burning thirst. In thoughtful mood we gazed around through the evening twilight. Far away on the western slope we could see some Kurdish women plodding along under heavy burdens of pine-branches like those that were now fumigating our eyes and nostrils. Across the hills the Kurdish shepherds were driving home their herds and flocks to the tinkling of bells. All this, to us, was deeply impressive. Such peaceful scenes, we thought, could never be the haunt of warlike robbers. The flocks at last came home; the shouts of the shepherds ceased; darkness fell; and all was quiet.

One by one the lights in the tents broke out, like the stars above. As the darkness deepened, they shone more and more brightly across the amphitheater of the encampment. The tent in which we were now sitting was oblong in shape, covered with a mixture of goats' and sheep's wool, carded, spun, and woven by the Kurdish women. This tenting was all of a dark brown or black color. The various strips were badly joined together, allowing the snow and rain, during the stormy night that followed, to penetrate plentifully. A wickerwork fencing, about three feet high, made from the reeds gathered in the swamps of the Aras River, was stretched around the bottom of the tent to keep out the cattle as well as to afford some little protection from the elements. This same material, of the same width or height, was used to partition off the apartments of the women. Far from being veiled and shut up in harems, like their Turkish and Persian sisters, the Kurdish women come and go among the men, and talk and laugh as they please. The thinness and lowness of the partition walls did not disturb their astonishing equanimity. In their relations with the men the women are extremely free. During the evening we frequently found ourselves surrounded by a concourse of these mountain beauties, who would sit and stare at us with their black eyes, call attention to our personal oddities, and laugh among themselves. Now and then their jokes at our expense would produce hilarious laughter among the men. The dress of these women consisted of baggy trousers, better described in this country as "divided skirts," a bright-colored overskirt and tunic, and a little round cloth cap encircled with a band of red and black. Through the right lobe of the nose was hung a peculiar button-shaped ornament studded with precious stones. This picturesque costume well set off their rich olive complexions, and black eyes beneath dark-brown lashes.

There were no signs of an approaching evening meal until we opened our provision-bag, and handed over certain articles of raw food to be cooked for us. No sooner were the viands intrusted to the care of our hosts, than two sets of pots and kettles made their appearance in the other compartments. In half an hour our host and friends proceeded to indulge their voracious appetites. When our own meal was brought to us some time after, we noticed that the fourteen eggs we had doled out had been reduced to six; and the other materials suffered a similar reduction, the whole thing being so patent as to make their attempt at innocence absurdly ludicrous. We thought, however, if Kurdish highway robbery took no worse form than this, we could well afford to be content. Supper over, we squatted round a slow-burning fire, on the thick felt mats which served as carpets, drank tea, and smoked the usual cigarettes. By the light of the glowing embers we could watch the faces about us, and catch their horrified glances when reference was made to our intended ascent of Ak-Dagh, the mysterious abode of the jinn. Before turning in for the night, we reconnoitered our situation. The lights in all the tents, save our own, were now extinguished. Not a sound was heard, except the heavy breathing of some of the slumbering animals about us, or the bark of a dog at some distant encampment. The huge dome of Ararat, though six to eight miles farther up the slope, seemed to be towering over us like some giant monster of another world. We could not see the summit, so far was it above the enveloping clouds. We returned to the tent to find that the zaptiehs had been given the best places and best covers to sleep in, and that we were expected to accommodate ourselves near the door, wrapped up in an old Kurdish carpet. Policy was evidently a better developed trait of Kurdish character than hospitality.

Although we arose at four, seven o'clock saw us still at the encampment. Two hours vanished before our gentlemen zaptiehs condescended to rise from their peaceful slumbers; then a great deal of time was unnecessarily consumed in eating their special breakfast. We ourselves had to be content with ekmek and yaourt (blotting-paper bread and curdled milk). This over, they concluded not to go on without sandals to take the place of their heavy military boots, as at this point their horses would have to be discarded. After we had employed a Kurd to make these for them, they declared they were afraid to proceed without the company of ten Kurds armed to the teeth. We knew that this was only a scheme on the part of the Kurds, with whom the zaptiehs were in league, to extort money from us. We still kept cool, and only casually insinuated that we did not have enough money to pay for so large a party. This announcement worked like a charm. The interest the Kurds had up to this time taken in our venture died away at once. Even the three Kurds who, as requested in the message of the mutessarif, were to accompany us up the mountain to the snow-line, refused absolutely to go. The mention of the mutessarif's name awakened only a sneer. We had also relied upon the Kurds for blankets, as we had been advised to do by our friends in Bayazid. Those we had already hired they now snatched from the donkeys standing before the tent. All this time our tall, gaunt, meek-looking muleteer had stood silent. Now his turn had come. How far was he to go with his donkeys?—he didn't think it possible for him to go much beyond this point. Patience now ceased to be a virtue. We cut off discussion at once; told the muleteer he would either go on, or lose what he had already earned; and informed the zaptiehs that whatever they did would be reported to the mutessarif on our return. Under this rather forcible persuasion, they stood not on the order of their going, but sullenly followed our little procession out of camp before the crestfallen Kurds.

In the absence of guides we were thrown upon our own resources. Far from being an assistance, our zaptiehs proved a nuisance. They would carry nothing, not even the food they were to eat, and were absolutely ignorant of the country we were to traverse. From our observations on the previous days, we had decided to strike out on a northeast course, over the gentle slope, until we struck the rocky ridges on the southeast buttress of the dome. On its projecting rocks, which extended nearer to the summit than those of any other part of the mountain, we could avoid the slippery, precipitous snow-beds that stretched far down the mountain at this time of the year.

Immediately after leaving the encampment, the ascent became steeper and more difficult; the small volcanic stones of yesterday now increased to huge obstructing boulders, among which the donkeys with difficulty made their way. They frequently tipped their loads, or got wedged in between two unyielding walls. In the midst of our efforts to extricate them, we often wondered how Noah ever managed with the animals from the ark. Had these donkeys not been of a philosophical turn of mind, they might have offered forcible objections to the way we extricated them from their straightened circumstances. A remonstrance on our part for carelessness in driving brought from the muleteer a burst of Turkish profanity that made the rocks of Ararat resound with indignant echoes. The spirit of insubordination seemed to be increasing in direct ratio with the height of our ascent.

We came now to a comparatively smooth, green slope, which led up to the highest Kurdish encampment met on the line of our ascent, about 7500 feet. When in sight of the black tents, the subject of Kurdish guides was again broached by the zaptiehs, and immediately they sat down to discuss the question. We ourselves were through with discussion, and fully determined to have nothing to do with a people who could do absolutely nothing for us. We stopped at the tents, and asked for milk. "Yes," they said; "we have some": but after waiting for ten minutes, we learned that the milk was still in the goats' possession, several hundred yards away among the rocks.

OUR GUARDS SIT DOWN TO DISCUSS THE SITUATION.
FRANCIS DAY.

It dawned upon us that this was only another trick of the zaptiehs to get a rest.

We pushed on the next 500 feet of the ascent without much trouble or controversy, the silence broken only by the muleteer, who took the *raki* bottle off the donkey's pack, and asked if he could take a drink. As we had only a limited supply, to be used to dilute the snow-water, we were obliged to refuse him.

At 8000 feet we struck our first snowdrift, into which the donkeys sank up to their bodies. It required our united efforts to lift them out, and half carry them across. Then on we climbed till ten o'clock, to a point about 9000 feet, where we stopped for lunch in a quiet mountain glen, by the side of a rippling mountain rill. This snow-water we drank with raki. The view in the mean time had been growing more and more extensive. The plain before us had lost nearly all its detail and color, and was merged into one vast whole. Though less picturesque, it was incomparably grander. Now we could see how, in ages past, the lava had burst out of the lateral fissures in the mountain, and flowed in huge streams for miles down the slope, and out on the plain below. These beds of lava were gradually broken up by the action of the elements, and now presented the appearance of ridges of broken volcanic rocks of the most varied and fantastic shapes.

It was here that the muleteer showed evident signs of weakening, which later on developed into a total collapse. We had come to a broad snow-field where the donkeys stuck fast and rolled over helpless in the snow. Even after we had unstrapped their baggage and carried it over on our shoulders, they could make no headway. The muleteer gave up in despair, and refused even to help us carry our loads to the top of an adjoining hill, whither the zaptiehs had proceeded to wait for us. In conse-

HELPING THE DONKEYS OVER A SNOW-FIELD.

quence, Raffl and we were compelled to carry two donkey-loads of baggage for half a mile over the snow-beds and boulders, followed by the sulking muleteer, who had deserted his donkeys, rather than be left alone himself. On reaching the zaptiehs, we sat down to hold a council on the situation; but the clouds, which, during the day, had occasionally obscured the top of the mountain, now began to thicken, and it was not long before a shower compelled us to beat a hasty retreat to a neighboring ledge of rocks. The clouds that were rolling between us and the mountain summit seemed but a token of the storm of circumstances. One thing was certain, the muleteer could go no farther up the mountain, and yet he was mortally afraid to return alone to the Kurdish robbers. He sat down, and began to cry like a child. This predicament of their accomplice furnished the zaptiehs with a plausible excuse. They now absolutely refused to go any farther without him. Our interpreter, the Greek, again joined the majority; he was not going to risk the ascent without the Turkish guards, and besides, he had now come to the conclusion that we had not sufficient blankets to spend a night at so high an altitude. Disappointed, but not discouraged, we gazed at the silent old gentleman at our side. In his determined countenance we read his answer. Long shall we remember Ignaz Raffl as one of the pluckiest, most persevering of old men.

There was now only one plan that could be pursued. Selecting from our supplies one small blanket, a felt mat, two long, stout ropes, enough food to last us two days, a bottle of cold tea, and a can of Turkish raki, we packed them into two bundles to strap on our backs. We then instructed the rest of the party to return to the Kurdish encampment and await our return. The sky was again clear at 2:30 P. M., when we bade good-by to our worthless comrades and resumed the ascent. We were now at a height of nine thousand feet, and it was our plan to camp at a point far enough up the mountain to enable us to complete the ascent on the following day, and return to the Kurdish encampment by nightfall. Beyond us was a region of snow and barren rocks, among which we still saw a small purple flower and bunches of lichens, which grew more rare as we advanced. Our course continued

LITTLE ARARAT COMES INTO VIEW.

in a northeast direction, toward the main southeast ridge of the mountain. Sometimes we were floundering with our heavy loads in the deep snow-beds, or scrambling on hands and knees over the huge boulders of the rocky seams. Two hours and a half of climbing brought us to the crest of the main southeast ridge, about one thousand feet below the base of the precipitous dome. At this point our course changed from northeast to northwest, and continued so during the rest of the ascent. Little Ararat was now in full view. We could even distinguish upon its northwest side a deep-cut gorge, which was not visible before. Upon its smooth and perfect slopes remained only the tatters of its last winter's garments. We could also look far out over the Sardarbulakh ridge, which connects the two Ararats, and on which the Cossacks are encamped. It was to them that the mutessarif had desired us to go, but we had subsequently determined to make the ascent directly from the Turkish side.

Following up this southeast ridge we came at 5 : 45 P. M. to a point about eleven thousand feet. Here the thermometer registered 39° Fahrenheit, and was constantly falling. If we should continue on, the cold during the night, especially with our scanty clothing, would become intolerable; and then, too, we could scarcely find a spot level enough to sleep on. We therefore determined to stop here for the night, and to continue the ascent at dawn. Some high, rugged crags on the ridge above us attracted our attention as affording a comparatively protected lodging. Among these we spread our carpet, and piled stones in the intervening spaces to form a complete inclosure. Thus busily engaged, we failed for a time to realize the grandeur of the situation. Over the vast and misty panorama that spread out before us, the lingering rays of the setting sun shed a tinge of gold, which was communicated to the snowy beds around us. Behind the peak of Little Ararat a brilliant rainbow stretched in one grand archway above the weeping clouds. But this was only one turn of nature's kaleidoscope. The arch soon faded away, and the shadows lengthened and deepened across the plain, and mingled, till all was lost to view behind the falling curtains of the night. The Kurdish tents far down the slope, and the white curling smoke from their evening camp-fires, we could see no more; only the occasional bark of a dog was borne upward through the impenetrable darkness.

Colder and colder grew the atmosphere. From 39° the thermometer gradually fell to 36°, to 33°, and during the night dropped below freezing-point. The snow, which fell from the clouds just over our heads, covered our frugal supper-table, on which were placed a few hard-boiled eggs, some tough Turkish bread, cheese, and a bottle of tea mixed with raki. Ice-tea was no doubt a luxury at this time of the year, but not on Mount Ararat, at the height of eleven thousand feet, with the temperature at freezing-point. M. Raffl was as cheerful as could be expected under the circumstances. He expressed his delight at our progress thus far; and now that we were free from our "gentlemen" attendants, he considered our chances for success much brighter. We turned in together under our single blanket, with the old gentleman between us. He had put on every article of clothing, including gloves, hat, hood, cloak, and heavy shoes. For pillows we used the provision-bags and camera. The bottle of cold tea we buttoned up in our coats to prevent it from freezing. On both sides, and above us, lay the pure white snow; below us a huge abyss, into which the rocky ridge descended like a darkened stairway to the lower regions. The awful stillness was unbroken, save by the whistling of the wind among the rocks. Dark masses of clouds seemed to bear down upon us every now and then, opening up their trap-doors, and letting down a heavy fall of snow. The heat of our bodies melted the ice beneath us, and our clothes became saturated with ice-water. Although we were surrounded by snow and ice, we were suffering with a burning thirst. Since separating from our companions we had found no water whatever, while the single bottle of cold

THE WALL INCLOSURE FOR OUR BIVOUAC AT ELEVEN THOUSAND FEET.

tea we had must be preserved for the morrow. Sleep, under such circumstances, and in our cramped position, was utterly impossible. At one o'clock the morning star peeped above the eastern horizon. This we watched hour after hour, as it rose in unrivaled beauty toward the zenith, until at last it began to fade away in the first gray streaks of the morning.

By the light of a flickering candle we ate a hurried breakfast, fastened on our spiked shoes, and strapped to our backs a few indispensable articles, leaving the rest of our baggage at the camp until our return. Just at daybreak, 3:55 A. M., on the 4th of July, we started off on what proved to be the hardest day's work we had ever accomplished. We struck out at once across the broad snow-field to the second rock rib on the right, which seemed to lead up to the only line of rocks above. The surface of these large snow-beds had frozen during the night, so that we had to cut steps with our ice-picks to keep from slipping down their glassy surface. Up this ridge we slowly climbed for three weary hours, leaping from boulder to boulder, or dragging ourselves up their precipitous sides. The old gentleman halted frequently to rest, and showed evident signs of weariness. "It is hard; we must take it slowly," he would say (in German) whenever our impatience would get the better of our prudence. At seven o'clock we reached a point about 13,500 feet, beyond which there seemed to be nothing but the snow-covered slope, with only a few projecting rocks along the edge of a tremendous gorge which now broke upon our astonished gaze. Toward this we directed our course, and, an hour later, stood upon its very verge. Our venerable companion now looked up at the precipitous slope above us, where only some stray, projecting rocks were left to guide us through the wilderness of snow.

"Boys," said he, despondently, "I cannot reach the top; I have not rested during the night, and I am now falling asleep on my feet; besides, I am very much fatigued." This came almost like a sob from a breaking heart. Al-

NEARING THE HEAD OF THE GREAT CHASM.

though the old gentleman was opposed to the ascent in the first instance, his old Alpine spirit arose within him with all its former vigor when once he had started up the mountain slope; and now, when almost in sight of the very goal, his strength began to fail him. After much persuasion and encouragement, he finally said that if he could get half an hour's rest and sleep, he thought he would be able to continue. We then wrapped him up in his greatcoat, and dug out a comfortable bed in the snow, while one of us sat down, with back against him, to keep him from rolling down the mountain-side.

We were now on the chasm's brink, looking down into its unfathomable depths. This gigantic rent, hundreds of feet in width and thousands in depth, indicates that northwest-southeast line along which the volcanic forces of Ararat have acted most powerfully. This fissure is perhaps the greatest with which the mountain is seamed, and out of which has undoubtedly been discharged a great portion of its lava. Starting from the base of the dome, it seemed to pierce the shifting clouds to a point about 500 feet from the summit. This line is continued out into the plain in a series of small volcanoes the craters of which appear to be as perfect as though they had been in activity only yesterday. The solid red and yellow rocks which lined the sides of the great chasm projected above the opposite brink in jagged and appalling cliffs. The whole was incased in a mass of huge fantastic icicles, which, glittering in the sunlight, gave it the appearance of a natural crystal palace. No more fitting place than this could the fancy of the Kurds depict for the home of the terrible jinn; no better symbol of nature for the awful jaws of death.

Our companion now awoke considerably refreshed, and the ascent was continued close to the chasm's brink. Here were the only rocks to be seen in the vast snow-bed around us. Cautiously we proceed, with cat-like tread, following directly in one another's footsteps, and holding on to our alpenstocks like grim death. A loosened rock would start at first slowly, gain momentum, and fairly fly. Striking against some projecting ledge, it would bound a hundred feet or more into the air, and then drop out of sight among the clouds below. Every few moments we would stop to rest; our knees were like lead, and the high altitude made breathing difficult. Now the trail of rocks led us within two feet of the chasm's edge; we approached it cautiously, probing well for a rock foundation, and gazing with dizzy heads into the abyss.

The slope became steeper and steeper, until it abutted in an almost precipitous cliff coated with snow and glistening ice. There was no escape from it, for all around the snow-beds were too steep and slippery to venture an ascent upon them. Cutting steps with our ice-picks, and half-crawling, half-dragging ourselves, with the alpenstocks hooked into the rocks above, we scaled its height, and advanced to the next abutment. Now a cloud, as warm as exhausted steam, enveloped us in the midst of this ice and snow. When it cleared away, the sun was reflected with intenser brightness. Our faces were already smarting with blisters, and our dark glasses afforded but little protection to our aching eyes.

At 11 A. M. we sat down on the snow to eat our last morsel of food. The cold chicken and bread tasted like sawdust, for we had no saliva with which to masticate them. Our single bottle of tea had given out, and we suffered with thirst for several hours. Again the word to start was given. We rose at once, but our stiffened legs quivered beneath us, and we leaned on our alpenstocks for support. Still we plodded on for two more weary hours, cutting our steps in the icy cliffs, or sinking to our thighs in the treacherous snow-beds. We could see that we were nearing the top of the great chasm, for the clouds, now entirely cleared away, left our view unobstructed. We could even descry the black Kurdish tents upon the northeast slope, and, far below, the Aras River, like a streak of silver, threading its way into the purple distance. The atmosphere about us grew colder, and we buttoned up our now too scanty garments. We must be nearing the top, we thought, and yet we were not certain, for a huge, precipitous cliff, just in front of us, cut off the view.

"Slowly, slowly," feebly shouted the old gentleman, as we began the attack on its precipitous sides, now stopping to brush away the treacherous snow, or to cut some steps in the solid ice. We pushed and pulled one another almost to the top, and then, with one more desperate effort, we stood upon a vast and gradually sloping snowbed. Down we plunged above our knees through the yielding surface, and staggered and fell with failing strength; then rose once more and plodded on, until at last we sank exhausted upon the top of Ararat.

For a moment only we lay gasping for breath; then a full realization of our situation dawned upon us, and fanned the few faint sparks of enthusiasm that remained in our exhausted bodies. We unfurled upon an alpenstock the small silk American flag that we had brought from home, and for the first time the "stars and stripes" was given to the breeze on the Mountain of the Ark. Four shots fired from our revolvers in commemoration of Independence Day broke the stillness of the gorges. Far above the clouds, which were rolling below us over three of the most absolute monarchies in the world, was celebrated in our simple way a great event of republicanism.

Mount Ararat, it will be observed from the accompanying sketch, has two tops, a few hundred yards apart, sloping, on the eastern and western extremities, into rather prominent abutments, and separated by a snow valley, or depression, from 50 to 100 feet in depth. The eastern top, on which we were standing, was quite extensive, and

ON THE SUMMIT OF MOUNT ARARAT — FIRING THE FOURTH OF JULY SALUTE.

30 to 40 feet lower than its western neighbor. Both tops are hummocks on the huge dome of Ararat, like the humps on the back of a camel, on neither one of which is there a vestige of anything but snow.

There remained just as little trace of the crosses left by Parrot and Chodzko, as of the ark itself. We remembered the pictures we had seen in our nursery-books, which represented this mountain-top covered with green grass, and Noah stepping out of the ark, in the bright, warm sunshine, before the receding waves; and now we looked around and saw this very spot covered with perpetual snow. Nor did we see any evidence whatever of a former existing crater, except perhaps the snow-filled depression we have just mentioned. There was nothing about this perpetual snow-field, and the freezing atmosphere that was chilling us to the bone, to remind us that we were on the top of an extinct volcano that once trembled with the convulsions of subterranean heat.

The view from this towering height was immeasurably extensive, and almost too grand. All detail was lost — all color, all outline; even the surrounding mountains seemed to be but excrescent ridges of the plain. Then, too, we could catch only occasional glimpses, as the clouds shifted to and fro. At one time they opened up beneath us, and revealed the Aras valley with its glittering ribbon of silver at an abysmal depth below. Now and then we could descry the black volcanic peaks of Ali Ghez forty miles away to the northwest, and on the southwest the low mountains that obscured the town of Bayazid. Of the Caucasus, the mountains about Erzerum on the west, and Lake Van on the south, and even of the Caspian Sea, all of which are said to be in Ararat's horizon, we could see absolutely nothing.

Had it been a clear day we could have seen not only the rival peaks of the Caucasus, which for so many years formed the northern wall of the civilized world, but, far to the south, we might have descried the mountains of Quardu land, where Chaldean legend has placed the landing of the ark. We might have gazed, in philosophic mood, over the whole of the Aras valley, which for 3000 years or more has been the scene of so much misery and conflict. As monuments of two extreme events in this historic period, two spots might have attracted our attention — one right below us, the ruins of Artaxata, which, according to tradition, was built, as the story goes, after the plans of the roving conqueror Hannibal, and stormed by the Roman legions, A. D. 58; and farther away to the north, the modern fortress of Kars, which so recently reverberated with the thunders of the Turkish war.

We were suddenly aroused by the rumbling of thunder below us. A storm was rolling rapidly up the southeast slope of the mountain. The atmosphere seemed to be boiling over the heated plain below. Higher and higher came the clouds, rolling and seething among the grim crags along the chasm; and soon we were caught in its embrace. The thermometer dropped at once below freezing-point, and the dense mists, driven against us by the hurricane, formed icicles on our blistered faces, and froze the ink in our fountain-pens. Our summer clothing was wholly inadequate for such an unexpected experience; we were chilled to the bone. To have remained where we were would have been jeopardizing our health, if not our lives. Although we could scarcely see far enough ahead to follow back on the track by which we had ascended, yet we were obliged to attempt it at once, for the storm around us was increasing every moment; we could even feel the charges of electricity whenever we touched the iron points of our alpenstocks.

Carefully peering through the clouds, we managed to follow the trail we had made along the gradually sloping summit, to the head of the great chasm, which now appeared more terrible than ever. We here saw that it would be extremely perilous, if not actually impossible, to attempt a descent on the rocks along its treacherous edge in such a hurricane. The only alternative was to take the precipitous snow-covered slope. Planting our ice-hooks deep in the snow behind us, we started. At first the strong head wind, which on the top almost took us off our feet, somewhat checked our downward career, but it was not long before we attained a velocity that made our hair stand on end. It was a thrilling experience; we seemed to be sailing through the air itself, for the clouds obscured the slope even twenty feet below. Finally we emerged beneath them into the glare of the afternoon sunlight; but on we dashed for 6000 feet, leaning heavily on the trailing-stocks, which threw up an icy spray in our wake. We never once stopped until we reached the bottom of the dome, at our last night's camp among the rocks.

In less than an hour we had dashed down through a distance which it had taken us nine and a half hours to ascend. The camp was reached at 4 P. M., just twelve hours from the time we left it. Gathering up the remaining baggage, we hurried away to continue the descent. We must make desperate efforts to reach the Kurdish encampment by nightfall; for during the last twenty-seven hours we had had nothing to drink but half a pint of tea, and our thirst by this time became almost intolerable.

The large snow-bed down which we had been sliding now began to show signs of treachery. The snow, at this low altitude, had melted out from below, to supply the subterranean streams, leaving only a thin crust at the surface. It was not long before one of our party fell into one of these pitfalls up to his shoulders, and floundered about for some time before he could extricate himself from his unexpected snow-bath.

Over the rocks and boulders the descent was much slower and more tedious. For two hours we were thus busily engaged, when all at once a shout rang out in the clear evening air. Looking up we saw, sure enough, our two zaptiehs and muleteer on the very spot where we had left them the evening before. Even the two donkeys were on hand to give us a welcoming bray. They had come up from the encampment early in the morning, and had been scanning the mountain all day long to get some clue to our whereabouts. They reported that they had seen us at one time during the morning, and had then lost sight of us among the clouds. This solicitude on their part was no doubt prompted by the fact that they were to be held by the mutessarif of Bayazid as personally responsible for our safe return, and perhaps, too, by the hope that they might thus retrieve the good graces they had lost the day before, and thereby increase the amount of the forthcoming baksheesh. Nothing, now, was too heavy for the donkeys, and even the zaptiehs themselves condescended to relieve us of our alpenstocks.

That night we sat again around the Kurdish camp-fire, surrounded by the same group of curious faces. It was interesting and even amusing to watch the bewildered astonishment that overspread their countenances as we related our experiences along the slope, and then upon the very top, of Ak-Dagh. They listened throughout with profound attention, then looked at one another in silence, and gravely shook their heads. They could not believe it. It was impossible. Old Ararat stood above us grim and terrible beneath the twinkling stars. To them it was, as it always will be, the same mysterious, untrodden height — the palace of the jinn.

III

THROUGH PERSIA TO SAMARKAND

"IT is all bosh," was the all but universal opinion of Bayazid in regard to our alleged ascent of Ararat. None but the Persian consul and the mutessarif himself deigned to profess a belief in it, and the gift of several letters to Persian officials, and a sumptuous dinner on the eve of our departure, went far toward proving their sincerity.

On the morning of July 8, in company with a bodyguard of zaptiehs, which the mutessarif forced upon us, we wheeled down from the ruined embattlements of Bayazid. The assembled rabble raised a lusty cheer at parting. An hour later we had surmounted the Kazlee Gool, and the "land of Iran" was before us. At our feet lay the Turco-Persian battle-plains of Chaldiran, spreading like a desert expanse to the parched barren hills beyond, and dotted here and there with clumps of trees in the village oases. And this, then, was the land where, as the poets say, "the nightingale sings, and the rose-tree blossoms," and where "a flower is crushed at every step!" More truth, we thought, in the Scotch traveler's description, which divides Persia into two portions — "One desert with salt, and the other desert without salt." In time we came to McGregor's opinion as expressed in his description of Khorassan. "We should fancy," said he, "a small green circle round every village indicated on the map, and shade all the rest in brown." The mighty hosts whose onward sweep from the Indus westward was checked only

HARVEST SCENE NEAR KHOI.

by the Grecian phalanx upon the field of Marathon must have come from the scattered ruins around, which reminded us that "Iran was; she is no more." Those myriad ranks of Yenghiz Khan and Tamerlane brought death and desolation from Turan to Iran, which so often met to act and react upon one another that both are now only landmarks in the sea of oblivion.

Our honorary escort accompanied us several miles over the border to the Persian village of Killissakend, and there committed us to the hospitality of the district khan, with whom we managed to converse in the Turkish language, which, strange to say, we found available in all the countries that lay in our transcontinental pathway as far as the great wall of China. Toward evening we rode in the garden of the harem of the khan, and at daybreak the next morning were again in the saddle. By a very early start we hoped to escape the burden of excessive hospitality; in other words, to get rid of an escort that was an expensive nuisance. At the next village we were confronted by what appeared to be a shouting, gesticulating maniac. On dismounting, we learned that a harbinger had been sent by the khan, the evening before, to have a guard ready to join us as we passed through. In fact, two armed *ferashes* were galloping toward us, armed, as we afterward learned, with American rifles, and the usual *kamma*, or huge dagger, swinging from a belt of cartridges. These fellows, like the zaptiehs, were fond of ostentation. They frequently led us a roundabout way to show us off to their relatives or friends in a neighboring village. Nature at last came to our deliverance. As we stood on a prominent ridge taking a last look at Mount Ararat, now more than fifty miles away, a storm came upon us, showering hailstones as large as walnuts. The ferashes with frantic steeds dashed ahead to seek a place of shelter, and we saw them no more.

Five days in Persia brought us to the shores of Lake Ooroomeeyah, the saltest body of water in the world. Early the next morning we were wading the chilly waters of the Hadji Chai, and a few hours later found us in the English consulate at Tabreez, where we were received by the Persian secretary. The English government, it seemed, had become embroiled in a local love-affair just at a time when Colonel Stewart was off on "diplomatic duty" on the Russian Transcaspian border. An exceptionally bright Armenian beauty, a graduate of the American missionary schools at this place, had been abducted, it was claimed,

by a young Kurdish cavalier, and carried away to his
mountain home. Her father, who happened to be a naturalized English subject, had applied for the assistance of
his adopted country in obtaining her release. Negotiations
were at once set on foot between London and Teheran,
which finally led to a formal demand upon the Kurds by
the Shah himself. Upon their repeated refusal, seven

LEAVING KHOI.

thousand Persian troops, it was said, were ordered to
Soak Boulak, under the command of the vice-consul, Mr.
Patton. The matter at length assumed such an importance as to give rise, in the House of Commons, to the
question, "Who is Katty Greenfield?" This, in time,
was answered by that lady herself, who declared under
oath that she had become a Mohammedan, and was in
love with the man with whom she had eloped. More

than this, it was learned that she had not a drop of English blood in her veins, her father being an Austrian, and her mother a native Armenian. Whereupon the Persian troopers, with their much disgusted leader, beat an inglorious retreat, leaving "Katty Greenfield" mistress of the situation, and of a Kurdish heart.

In Tabreez there is one object sure to attract attention. This is the "Ark," or ancient fortified castle of the Persian rulers. High on one of the sides, which a recent earthquake has rent from top to bottom, there is a little porch whence these Persian "Bluebeards," or rather Redbeards, were wont to hurl unruly members of the harem. Under the shadow of these gloomy walls was enacted a tragedy of this century. Babism is by no means the only heresy that has sprung from the speculative genius of Persia; but it is the one that has most deeply moved the society of the present age, and the one which still obtains, though in secret and without a leader. Its founder, Seyd Mohammed Ali, better known as Bab, or "Gate," promulgated the doctrine of anarchy to the extent of "sparing the rod and spoiling the child," and still worse, perhaps, of refusing to the ladies no finery that might be at all becoming to their person. While not a communist, as he has sometimes been wrongly classed, he exhorted the wealthy to regard themselves as only trustees of the poor. With no thought at first of acquiring civil power, he and his rapidly increasing following were driven to revolt by the persecuting mollas, and the sanguinary struggle of 1848 followed. Bab himself was captured, and carried to this "most fanatical city of Persia," the burial-place of the sons of Ali. On this very spot a company was ordered to despatch him with a volley; but when the smoke cleared away, Bab was not to be seen. None of the bullets had gone to the mark, and the bird had flown

YARD OF CARAVANSARY AT TABREEZ.

LUMBER-YARD AT TABREEZ.

—but not to the safest refuge. Had he finally escaped, the miracle thus performed would have made Babism invincible. But he was recaptured and despatched, and his body thrown to the canine scavengers.

Tabreez (fever-dispelling) was a misnomer in our case. Our sojourn here was prolonged for more than a month by a slight attack of typhoid fever, which this time seized Sachtleben, and again the kind nursing of the missionary ladies hastened recovery. Our mail, in the mean time, having been ordered to Teheran, we were granted the privilege of intercepting it. For this purpose we were permitted to overhaul the various piles of letters strewn over the dirty floor of the distributing-office. Both the Turkish and Persian mail is carried in saddle-bags on the backs of reinless horses driven at a rapid gallop before the mounted mail-carrier or herdsman. Owing to the carelessness of the postal officials, legations and consulates employ special couriers.

The proximity of Tabreez to the Russian border makes it politically, as well as commercially, one of the most important cities in Persia. For this reason it is the place of residence of the Emir-e-Nizam (leader of the army), or prime minister, as well as the Vali-Ahd, or Prince Imperial. This prince is the Russian candidate, as opposed to the English candidate, for the prospective vacancy on the throne. Both of these dignitaries invited us to visit them, and showed much interest in our "wonderful wind horses," of the speed of which exaggerated reports had circulated through the country. We were also favored with a special letter for the journey to the capital.

On this stage we started August 15, stopping the first night at Turkmanchai, the little village where was signed the famous treaty of 1828 by virtue of which the Caspian Sea became a Russian lake. The next morning we were on the road soon after daybreak, and on approaching the next village overtook a curious cavalcade, just concluding a long night's journey. This consisted of a Persian palanquin, with its long pole-shafts saddled upon the back of a mule at each end; with servants on foot, and a body-guard of mounted soldiers. The occupant of this peculiar conveyance remained concealed throughout the stampede which our sudden appearance occasioned among his hearse-bearing mules, for as such they will appear in the sequel. In our first article we mentioned an interview in London with Malcolm Khan, the representative of the Shah at the court of St. James. Since then, it seemed, he had fallen into disfavor. During the late visit of the Shah to England certain members of his retinue were so young, both in appearance and conduct, as to be a source of mortification to the Europeanized minister. This reached the ears of the Shah some time after his return home; and a summons was sent for the accused to repair to Teheran. Malcolm Khan, however, was too well versed in Oriental craft to fall into such a trap, and announced his purpose to devote his future leisure to airing his knowledge of Persian politics in the London press. The Persian Minister of Foreign Affairs, Musht-a-Shar-el-Dowlet, then residing at Tabreez, who was accused of carrying on a seditious correspondence with Malcolm Khan, was differently situated, unfortunately. It was during our sojourn in that city that his palatial household was raided by a party of soldiers, and he was carried to prison as a common felon. Being unable to pay the high price of pardon that was demanded, he was forced away, a few days before our departure, on that dreaded journey to the capital, which few, if any, ever complete. For on the way they are usually met by a messenger, who proffers them a cup of coffee, a sword, and a rope, from which they are to choose the method of their doom. This, then, was the occupant of the mysterious palanquin, which now was opened as we drew up before the village caravansary. Out stepped a man, tall and portly, with beard and hair

THE CONVEYANCE OF A PERSIAN OFFICIAL TRAVELING IN DISGRACE TO TEHERAN AT THE CALL OF THE SHAH.

of venerable gray. His keen eye, clear-cut features, and dignified bearing, bespoke for him respect even in his downfall, while his stooped shoulders and haggard countenance betrayed the weight of sorrow and sleepless nights with which he was going to his tomb.

At Miana, that town made infamous by its venomous insect, is located one of the storage-stations of the Indo-European Telegraph Company. Its straight lines of iron poles, which we followed very closely from Tabreez to Teheran, form only a link in that great wire and cable chain which connects Melbourne with London. We spent the following night in the German operator's room.

The weakness of the Persian for mendacity is proverbial. One instance of this national weakness was attended with considerable inconvenience to us. By some mischance we had run by the village where we intended to stop for the night, which was situated some distance off the road. Meeting a Persian lad, we inquired the distance. He was ready at once with a cheerful falsehood. "One farsak" (four miles), he replied, although he must have known at the time that the village was already behind us. On we pedaled at an increased rate, in order to precede, if possible, the approaching darkness; for although traditionally the land of a double dawn, Persia has only one twilight, and that closely merged into sunset and darkness. One, two farsaks were placed behind us, and still there was no sign of a human habitation. At length darkness fell; we were obliged to dismount to feel our way. By the gradually rising ground, and the rocks, we knew we were off the road. Dropping our wheels, we groped round on hands and knees, to find, if possible, some trace of water. With a burning thirst, a chilling atmosphere, and swarms of mosquitos biting through our clothing, we could not sleep. A slight drizzle began to descend. During our gloomy vigil we were glad to hear the sounds of a caravan, toward which we groped our way, discerning, at length, a long line of camels marching to the music of their lantern-bearing leader. When our nickel-plated bars and white helmets flashed in the lantern-light, there was a shriek, and the lantern fell to the ground. The rear-guard rushed to the front with drawn weapons; but even they started back at the sound of our voices, as we attempted in broken Turkish to reassure them. Explanations were made, and the camels soon quieted. Thereupon we were surrounded with lanterns and firebrands, while the remainder of the caravan party was called to the front. Finally we moved on, walking side by side with the lantern-bearing leader, who ran ahead now and then to make sure of the road. The night was the blackest we had ever seen. Suddenly one of the camels disappeared in a ditch, and rolled over with a groan. Fortunately, no bones were broken, and the load was replaced. But we were off the road, and a search was begun with lights to find the beaten path. Footsore and hungry, with an almost intolerable thirst, we trudged along till morning, to the ding-dong, ding-dong of the deep-toned camel-bells. Finally we reached a sluggish river, but did not dare to satisfy our thirst, except by washing out our mouths, and by taking occasional swallows, with long intervals of rest, in one of which we fell asleep from sheer exhaustion. When we awoke the midday sun was shining, and a party of Persian travelers was bending over us.

From the high lands of Azerbeidjan, where, strange to say, nearly all Persian pestilences arise, we dropped suddenly into the Kasveen plain, a portion of that triangular, dried-up basin of the Persian Mediterranean, now for the most part a sandy, saline desert. The argillaceous dust accumulated on the Kasveen plain by the weathering of the surrounding uplands resembles in appearance the "yellow earth" of the Hoang Ho district in China, but remains sterile for the lack of water. Even the little moisture that obtains beneath the surface is sapped by the *kanots*, or underground canals, which bring to the fevered lips of the desert oases the fresh, cool springs of the Elburz. These are dug with unerring instinct, and preserved with jealous care by means of shafts or slanting wells dug at regular intervals across the plain. Into these we would occasionally descend to relieve our reflection-burned — or, as a Persian would say, "snow-burned" — faces, while the thermometer above stood at 120° in the shade.

Over the level ninety-mile stretch between Kasveen and the capital a so-called carriage-road has recently been constructed close to the base of the mountain. A sudden turn round a mountain-spur, and before us was presented to view Mount Demavend and Teheran. Soon the paved streets, sidewalks, lamp-posts, street-railways, and even steam-tramway, of the half modern capital were as much of a surprise to us as our " wind horses" were to the curious crowds that escorted us to the French Hotel.

From Persia it was our plan to enter Russian central Asia, and thence to proceed to China or Siberia. To enter

A PERSIAN REPAIRING THE WHEELS OF HIS WAGON.

the Transcaspian territory, the border-province of the Russian possessions, the sanction of its governor, General Kuropatkine, would be quite sufficient; but for the rest of the journey through Turkestan the Russian minister in Teheran said we would have to await a general permission from St. Petersburg. Six weeks were spent with our English and American acquaintances, and still no answer was received. Winter was coming on, and something had to be done at once. If we were to be debarred from a northern route, we would have to attempt a passage into India either through Afghanistan, which we were assured by all was quite impossible, or across the deserts of southern Persia and Baluchistan. For this latter we had already obtained a possible route from the noted traveler, Colonel Stewart, whom we met on his way back to his consular post at Tabreez. But just at this juncture the Russian minister advised another plan. In order to save time, he said, we might proceed to Meshed at once, and if our permission was not telegraphed to us at that point, we could then turn south to Ba' chistan as a last resort. This, our friends unanimously declared, was a Muscovite trick to evade an absolute re   Russians, they assured us, would never per   gn inspection of their doings on the Afgh   r; nd furthermore, we would never be able to   the   in-habited deserts of Baluchistan. Against all prot   e waved "farewell" to the foreign and native throng   1 had assembled to see us off, and on October 5 wheeled of the fortified square on the "Pilgrim Road to Meshed."

Before us now lay six hundred miles of barren hills, swampy *kevirs,* brier-covered wastes, and salty deserts, with here and there some kanot-fed oases. To the south lay the lifeless desert of Luth, the "Persian Sahara," the humidity of which is the lowest yet recorded on the face of the globe, and compared with which "the Gobi of China and the Kizil-Kum of central Asia are fertile regions." It is our extended and rather unique experience on the former of these two that prompts us to refrain from further description of desert travel here, where the hardships were in a measure ameliorated by frequent stations, and by the use of cucumbers and pomegranates, both of which we carried with us on the long desert stretches. Melons,

TRAINING SCHOOL AT MEERUT.

too, the finest we have ever seen in any land, frequently obviated the necessity of drinking the strongly brackish water.

Yet this experience was sufficient to impress us with the fact that the national poets, Hafiz and Sadi, like Thomas Moore, have sought in fancy what the land of Iran denied them. Those "spicy groves, echoing with the nightingale's song," those "rosy bowers and purling brooks," on the whole exist, so far as our experience goes, only in the poet's dream.

Leaving on the right the sand-swept ruins of Veramin, that capital of Persia before Teheran was even thought of, we traversed the pass of Sir-Dara, identified by some as the famous "Caspian Gate," and early in the evening entered the village of Aradan. The usual crowd hemmed us in on all sides, yelling, "Min, min!" ("Ride, ride!"), which took the place of the Turkish refrain of "Bin, bin!" As we rode toward the caravansary they shouted, "Faster, faster!" and when we began to distance them, they caught at the rear wheels, and sent a shower of stones after us, denting our helmets, and bruising our coatless backs. This was too much; we dismounted and exhibited the ability to defend ourselves, whereupon they tumbled over one another in their haste to get away. But they were at our wheels again before we reached the caravansary. Here they surged through the narrow gangway, and knocked over the fruit-stands of the bazaars.

We were shown to a room, or windowless cell, in the honeycomb structure that surrounded an open quadrangular court, at the time filled with a caravan of pilgrims, carrying triangular white and black flags, with the Persian coat of arms, the same we have seen over many doorways in Persia as warnings of the danger of trespassing upon the religious services held within. The cadaverous stench revealed the presence of half-dried human bones being carried by relatives and friends for interment in the sacred "City of the Silent." Thus dead bodies, in loosely

IN A PERSIAN GRAVEYARD.

nailed boxes, are always traveling from one end of Persia to the other. Among the pilgrims were blue and green turbaned Saids, direct descendants of the Prophet, as well as white-turbaned mollas. All were sitting about on the *sakoo*, or raised platform, just finishing the evening meal. But presently one of the mollas ascended the mound in the middle of the stable-yard, and in the manner of the muezzin called to prayer. All kneeled, and bowed their heads toward Mecca. Then the horses were saddled, the long, narrow boxes attached upright to the pack-mules, and the *kajavas*, or double boxes, adjusted on the backs of the horses of the ladies. Into these the veiled creatures entered, and drew the curtains, while the men leaped into the saddle at a signal, and, with the tri-cornered flag at their head, the cavalcade moved out on its long night pilgrimage. We now learned that the village contained a *chappar khan*, one of those places of rest which have recently been provided for the use of foreigners and others, who travel *chappar*, or by relays of post-horses. These structures are usually distinguished by a single room built on the roof, and projecting some distance over the eaves.

To this we repaired at once. Its keeper evinced unusual pride in the cleanliness of his apartments, for we were asked to take off our shoes before entering. But while our boastful host was kicking up the mats to convince us of the truth of his assertions, he suddenly retired behind the scenes to rid himself of some of the pests.

Throughout our Asiatic tour eggs were our chief means of subsistence, but *pillao*, or boiled rice flavored with grease, we found more particularly used in Persia, like

PILGRIMS IN THE CARAVANSARY.

yaourt in Turkey. This was prepared with chicken whenever it was possible to purchase a fowl, and then we would usually make the discovery that a Persian fowl was either wingless, legless, or otherwise defective after being prepared by a Persian *fuzul,* or foreigner's servant, who, it is said, "shrinks from no baseness in order to eat." Though minus these particular appendages, it would invariably have a head; for the fanatical Shiah frequently snatched

A PERSIAN WINE-PRESS.

a chicken out of our hands to prevent us from wringing or chopping its head off. Even after our meal was served, we would keep a sharp lookout upon the unblushing pilferers around us, who had called to pay their respects, and to fill the room with clouds of smoke from their chibouks and gurgling kalians. For a fanatical Shiah will sometimes stick his dirty fingers into the dishes of an "unbeliever," even though he may subsequently throw away the contaminated vessel. And this extreme fanaticism is to be found in a country noted for its extensive latitude in the profession of religious beliefs.

A present from the village khan was announced. In stepped two men bearing a huge tray filled with melons, apricots, sugar, rock-candy, nuts, pistachios, etc., all of which we must, of course, turn over to the khan-keeper and his servants, and pay double their value to the bearers, as a present. This polite method of extortion was followed the next morning by one of a bolder and more peremptory nature. Notwithstanding the feast of the night before at our expense, and in addition to furnishing us with bedclothes which we really ought to have been paid to sleep in, our oily host now insisted upon three or four prices for his lodgings. We refused to pay him more than a certain sum, and started to vacate the premises. Thereupon he and his grown son caught hold of our bicycles. Remonstrances proving of no avail, and being unable to force our passage through the narrow doorway with the bicycles in our hands, we dropped them, and grappled with our antagonists. A noisy scuffle, and then a heavy fall ensued, but luckily we were both on the upper side. This unusual disturbance now brought out the inmates of the adjoining *anderoon*. In a moment there was a din of feminine screams, and a flutter of garments, and then — a crashing of our pith helmets beneath the blows of pokers and andirons. The villagers, thus aroused, came at last to our rescue, and at once proceeded to patch up a compromise. This, in view of the Amazonian reinforcements, who were standing by in readiness for a second onset, we were more than pleased to accept. From this inglorious combat we came off without serious injury; but with those gentle poker taps were knocked out forever all the sweet delusions of the "Light of the Harem."

The great antiquity of this Teheran-Meshed road, which is undoubtedly a section of that former commercial highway between two of the most ancient capitals in history

—Nineveh and Balk, is very graphically shown by the caravan ruts at Lasgird. These have been worn in many places to a depth of four feet in the solid rock. It was not far beyond this point that we began to feel the force of that famous "Damghan wind," so called from the city of that name. Of course this wind was against us. In fact, throughout our Asiatic tour easterly winds prevailed;

CASTLE STRONGHOLD AT LASGIRD.

and should we ever attempt another transcontinental spin we would have a care to travel in the opposite direction.

Our peculiar mode of travel subjected us to great extremes in our mode of living. Sometimes, indeed, it was a change almost from the sublime to the ridiculous, and vice versa — from a stable or sheepfold, with a diet of figs and bread, and an irrigating-ditch for a lavatory, to a palace itself, an Oriental palace, with all the delicacies of the East, and a host of servants to attend to our slightest wish. So it was at Bostam, the residence of one of Persia's most influential *hakims*, or governors, literally, "pillars of state," who was also a cousin to the Shah himself. This potentate we visited in company with an English engineer whom we met in transit at Sharoud. It was on the evening before, when at supper with this gentleman in his tent, that a special messenger arrived from the governor, requesting us, as the invitation ran, "to take our brightness into his presence." As we entered, the governor rose from his seat on the floor, a courtesy never shown us by a Turkish official. Even the politest of them would, just at this particular moment, be conveniently engrossed in the examination of some book or paper. His courtesy was further extended by locking up our "horses," and making us his "prisoners" until the following morning. At the dinner which Mr. Evans and we were invited to eat with his excellency, benches had to be especially prepared, as there was nothing like a chair to be found on the premises. The governor himself took his accustomed position on the floor, with his own private dishes around him. From these he would occasionally fish out with his fingers some choice lamb *kebabh* or cabbage *dolmah*, and have it passed over to his guests—an act which is considered one of the highest forms of Persian hospitality.

With a shifting of the scenes of travel, we stood at sunset on the summit of the Binalud mountains, overlooking the valley of the Kashafrud. Our two weeks' journey was almost ended, for the city of Meshed was now in view, ten miles away. Around us were piles of little stones, to which each pious pilgrim adds his quota when first he sees the "Holy Shrine," which we beheld shining like a ball of fire in the glow of the setting sun.

While we were building our pyramid a party of returning pilgrims greeted us with "Meshedi at last." "Not yet," we answered, for we knew that the gates of the Holy City closed promptly at twilight. Yet we determined to make the attempt. On we sped, but not with the speed of the

PILGRIM STONE HEAPS OVERLOOKING MESHED.

falling night. Dusk overtook us as we reached the plain. A moving form was revealed to us on the bank of the irrigating-canal which skirted the edge of the road. Backward it fell as we dashed by, and then the sound of a splash and splutter reached us as we disappeared in the darkness. On the morrow we learned that the spirits of Hassan and Hussein were seen skimming the earth in their flight toward the Holy City. We reached the bridge, and crossed the moat, but the gates were closed. We knocked and pounded, but a hollow echo was our only response. At last the light of a lantern illumined the crevices in the weather-beaten doors, and a weird-looking face appeared through the midway opening. "Who's there?" said a voice, whose sepulchral tones might have belonged to the sexton of the Holy Tomb. "We are *Ferenghis*," we said, "and must get into the city to-night." "That is impossible," he answered, "for the gates are locked, and the keys have been sent away to the governor's palace." With this the night air grew more chill. But another thought struck us at once. We would send a note to General McLean, the English consul-general, who was already expecting us. This our interlocutor, for a certain *inam*, or Persian bakshish, at length agreed to deliver. The general, as we afterward learned, sent a servant with a special request to the governor's palace. Here, without delay, a squad of horsemen was detailed, and ordered with the keys to the "Herat Gate." The crowds in the streets, attracted by this unusual turnout at this unusual hour, followed in their wake to the scene of disturbance. There was a click

RIDING BEFORE THE GOVERNOR AT MESHED.

of locks, the clanking of chains, and the creaking of rusty hinges. The great doors swung open, and a crowd of expectant faces received us in the Holy City.

Meshed claims our attention chiefly for its famous dead. In its sacred dust lie buried our old hero Haroun al Raschid, Firdousi, Persia's greatest epic poet, and the holy Imaum

Riza, within whose shrine every criminal may take refuge from even the Shah himself until the payment of a blood-tax, or a debtor until the giving of a guarantee for debt. No infidel can enter there.

Meshed was the pivotal point upon which our wheel of fortune was to turn. We were filled with no little anxiety, therefore, when, on the day after our arrival, we received an invitation to call at the Russian consulate-general. With great ceremony we were ushered into a suite of elegantly furnished rooms, and received by the consul-general and his English wife in full dress. Madame de Vlassow was radiant with smiles as she served us tea by the side of her steaming silver samovar. She could not wait for

FEMALE PILGRIMS ON THE ROAD TO MESHED.

the circumlocution of diplomacy, but said: "It is all right, gentlemen. General Kuropatkine has just telegraphed permission for you to proceed to Askabad." This precipitate remark evidently disconcerted the consul, who could only nod his head and say, "*Oui, oui*," in affirmation. This news lifted a heavy load from our minds; our desert

IN THE GARDEN OF THE RUSSIAN CONSULATE AT MESHED.

journey of six hundred miles, therefore, had not been made in vain, and the prospect brightened for a trip through the heart of Asia.

Between the rival hospitality of the Russian and English consulates our health was now in jeopardy from excess of kindness. Among other social attentions, we received an invitation from Sahib Devan, the governor of Khorassan, who next to the Shah is the richest man in Persia. Although seventy-six years of age, on the day of our visit to his palace he was literally covered with diamonds and precious stones. With the photographer to the Shah as German interpreter, we spent half an hour in an interesting conversation. Among other topics he mentioned the receipt, a few days before, of a peculiar telegram from the Shah: "Cut off the head of any one who attempts opposition to the Tobacco Regie"; and this was followed a few days after by the inquiry, "How many heads have you taken?" A retinue of about three hundred courtiers followed the governor as he walked out with feeble steps

WATCH-TOWER ON THE TRANSCASPIAN RAILWAY.

to the parade-ground. Here a company of Persian cavalry was detailed to clear the field for the "wonderful steel horses," which, as was said, had come from the capital in two days, a distance of six hundred miles. The governor's extreme pleasure was afterward expressed in a special letter for our journey to the frontier.

The military road now completed between Askabad and Meshed reveals the extreme weakness of Persia's defense against Russian aggression. Elated by her recent successes in the matter of a Russian consul at Meshed, Russia

GIVING A "SILENT PILGRIM" A ROLL TOWARD MESHED.

has very forcibly invited Persia to construct more than half of a road which, in connection with the Transcaspian railway, makes Khorassan almost an exclusive Russian market, and opens Persia's richest province to Russia's troops and cannon on the prospective march to Herat. At this very writing, if the telegraph speaks the truth, the Persian border-province of Dereguez is another cession by what the Russians are pleased to call their Persian vassal. In addition to its increasing commercial traffic, this road is patronized by many Shiah devotees from the north, among whom are what the natives term the "silent pilgrims." These are large stones, or boulders, rolled along a few feet at a time by the passers-by toward the Holy City. We ourselves were employed in this pious work at the close of our first day's journey from Meshed when we were suddenly aroused by a bantering voice behind us. Looking up, we were hailed by Stagno Navarro, the inspector of the Persian telegraph, who was employed with his men on a neighboring line. With this gentleman we spent the following night in a telegraph station, and passed a pleasant evening chatting over the wires with friends in Meshed.

Kuchan, our next stopping-place, lies on the almost imperceptible watershed which separates the Herat valley from the Caspian Sea. This city, only a few months ago, was entirely destroyed by a severe earthquake. Under date of January 28, 1894, the American press reported: "The bodies of ten thousand victims of the awful disaster have already been recovered. Fifty thousand cattle were destroyed at the same time. The once important and beautiful city of twenty thousand people is now only a scene of death, desolation, and terror."

From this point to Askabad the construction of the military highway speaks well for Russia's engineering skill. It crosses the Kopet Dagh mountains over seven distinct passes in a distance of eighty miles. This we determined to cover, if possible, in one day, inasmuch as there was no intermediate stopping-place, and as we were not a little delighted by the idea of at last emerging from semi-barbarism into semi-civilization. At sunset we were scaling the fifth ridge since leaving Kuchan at daybreak, and a few minutes later rolled up before the Persian custom-house in the valley below. There was no evidence of the proximity of a Russian frontier, except the extraordinary size of the tea-glasses, from which we slaked our intolerable thirst. During the day we had had a surfeit of cavernous gorges and commanding pinnacles, but very little water. The only copious spring we were able to find was filled at the time with the unwashed linen of a

Persian traveler, who sat by, smiling in derision, as we upbraided him for his disregard of the traveling public.

It was already dusk when we came in sight of the Russian custom-house, a tin-roofed, stone structure, contrasting strongly with the Persian mud hovels we had left behind. A Russian official hailed us as we shot by, but we could not stop on the down-grade, and, besides, darkness

AN INTERVIEW WITH GENERAL KUROPATKINE AT THE RACES NEAR ASKABAD.

was too rapidly approaching to brook any delay. Askabad was twenty-eight miles away, and although wearied by an extremely hard day's work, we must sleep that night, if possible, in a Russian hotel. Our pace increased with the growing darkness until at length we were going at the rate of twelve miles per hour down a narrow gorge-like valley toward the seventh and last ridge that lay between us and the desert. At 9:30 P. M. we stood upon its summit, and before us stretched the sandy wastes of Kara-Kum, enshrouded in gloom. Thousands of feet below us the city of Askabad was ablaze with lights, shining like beacons on the shore of the desert sea. Strains of music from a Russian band stole faintly up through the darkness as we dismounted, and contemplated the strange scene,

MOSQUE CONTAINING THE TOMB OF TAMERLANE AT SAMARKAND.

until the shriek of a locomotive-whistle startled us from our reveries. Across the desert a train of the Transcaspian railway was gliding smoothly along toward the city.

A hearty welcome back to civilized life was given us the next evening by General Kuropatkine himself, the Governor-General of Transcaspia. During the course of a dinner with him and his friends, he kindly assured us that no further recommendation was needed than the fact that we were American citizens to entitle us to travel from one end of the Russian empire to the other.

From Askabad to Samarkand there was a break in the continuity of our bicycle journey. Our Russian friends persuaded us to take advantage of the Transcaspian railway, and not to hazard a journey across the dreaded Kara-Kum sands. Such a journey, made upon the railroad track, where water and food were obtainable at regular intervals, would have entailed only a small part of the hardships incurred on the deserts in China, yet we were more than anxious to reach, before the advent of winter, a point whence we could be assured of reaching the Pacific during the following season. Through the kindness of the railway authorities at Bokhara station our car was side-tracked to enable us to visit, ten miles away, that ancient city of the East. On November 6 we reached Samarkand, the ancient capital of Tamerlane, and the present terminus of the Transcaspian railway.

CARAVANSARY AT FAKIDAOUD.

A MARKET-PLACE IN SAMARKAND, AND THE RUINS OF A COLLEGE.

IV

THE JOURNEY FROM SAMARKAND TO KULDJA

ON the morning of November 16 we took a last look at the blue domes and minarets of Samarkand, intermingled with the ruins of palaces and tombs, and then wheeled away toward the banks of the Zerafshan. Our four days' journey of 180 miles along the regular Russian post-road was attended with only the usual vicissitudes of ordinary travel. Wading in our Russian top-boots through the treacherous fords of the "Snake" defile, we passed the pyramidal slate rock known as the "Gate of Tamerlane," and emerged upon a strip of the Kizil-Kum steppe, stretching hence in painful monotony to the bank of the Sir Daria river. This we crossed by a rude rope-ferry, filled at the time with a passing caravan, and then began at once to ascend the valley of the Tchirtchick toward Tashkend. The blackened cotton which the natives were gathering from the fields, the lowering snow-line on the mountains, the muddy roads, the chilling atmosphere, and the falling leaves of the giant poplars—all warned us of the approach of winter.

We had hoped at least to reach Vernoye, a provincial capital near the converging point of the Turkestan, Siberian, and Chinese boundaries, whence we could continue, on the opening of the following spring, either through

Siberia or across the Chinese empire. But in this we were doomed to disappointment. The delay on the part of the Russian authorities in granting us permission to enter Transcaspia had postponed at least a month our

A RELIGIOUS DRAMA IN SAMARKAND.

arrival in Tashkend, and now, owing to the early advent of the rainy season, the roads leading north were almost impassable even for the native carts. This fact, together with the reports of heavy snowfalls beyond the Alexandrovski mountains, on the road to Vernoye, lent a rather cogent influence to the persuasions of our friends to spend the winter among them.

Then, too, such a plan, we thought, might not be unproductive of future advantages. Thus far we had been journeying through Russian territory without a passport. We had no authorization except the telegram to "come on," received from General Kuropatkine at Askabad, and the verbal permission of Count Rosterzsoff at Samarkand to proceed to Tashkend. Furthermore, the passport for which we had just applied to Baron Wrevsky, the Governor-General of Turkestan, would be available only as far as the border of Siberia, where we should have to apply to the various governors-general along our course to the Pacific, in case we should find the route across the Chinese empire impracticable. A general permission to travel from Tashkend to the Pacific coast, through southern Siberia, could be obtained from St. Petersburg only, and that only through the chief executive of the province through which we were passing.

Permission to enter Turkestan is by no means easily obtained, as is well understood by the student of Russian policy in central Asia. We were not a little surprised, therefore, when our request to spend the winter in its capital was graciously granted by Baron Wrevsky, as well as the privilege for one of us to return in the mean time to London. This we had determined on, in order to secure some much-needed bicycle supplies, and to complete other arrangements for the success of our enterprise. By lot the return trip fell to Sachtleben. Proceeding by the Transcaspian and Transcaucasus railroads, the Caspian and Black seas, to Constantinople, and thence by the "overland express" to Belgrade, Vienna, Frankfort, and Calais, he was able to reach London in sixteen days.

Tashkend, though nearly in the same latitude as New York, is so protected by the Alexandrovski mountains from the Siberian blizzards and the scorching winds of the Kara-Kum desert as to have an even more moderate climate. A tributary of the Tchirtchick river forms the line of demarcation between the native and the European portions of the city, although the population of the latter is by no means devoid of a native element. Both together cover an area as extensive as Paris, though the population is only 120,000, of which 100,000 are congregated in the native, or Sart, quarter. There is a floating element of Kashgarians, Bokhariots, Persians, and Afghans, and a resident majority of Kirghiz, Tatars, Jews, Hindus, gypsies,

OUR FERRY OVER THE ZERAFSHAN.

and Sarts, the latter being a generic title for the urban, as distinguished from the nomad, people.

Our winter quarters were obtained at the home of a typical Russian family, in company with a young reserve officer. He, having finished his university career and time of military service, was engaged in Tashkend in the interest of his father, a wholesale merchant in Moscow. With him we were able to converse either in French or German, both of which languages he could speak more purely than his native Russian. Our good-natured, corpulent host had emigrated, in the pioneer days, from the steppes of southern Russia, and had grown wealthy through the "unearned increment."

The Russian samovar is the characteristic feature of the Russian household. Besides a big bowl of cabbage soup at every meal, our Russian host would start in with a half-tumbler of vodka, dispose of a bottle of beer in the intervals, and then top off with two or three glasses of tea. The mistress of the household, being limited in her beverages to tea and soup, would usually make up in quantity what was lacking in variety. In fact, one day she informed us that she had not imbibed a drop of water for over six years. For this, however, there is a very plausible excuse. With the water at Tashkend, as with that from the Zerafshan at Bokhara, a dangerous worm called *reshta* is absorbed into the system. Nowhere have we drunk better tea than around the steaming samovar of our Tashkend host. No peasant is too poor, either in money or in sentiment, to buy and feel the cheering influence of tea. Even the Cossack, in his forays into the wilds of central Asia, is sustained by it. Unlike the Chinese, the Russians consider sugar a necessary concomitant of tea-drinking. There are three methods of sweetening tea: to put the sugar in the glass; to place a lump of sugar in the mouth, and suck the tea through it; to hang a lump in the midst of a tea-drinking circle, to be swung around for each in turn to touch with his tongue, and then to take a swallow of tea.

The meaning of the name Tashkend is "city of stone," but a majority of the houses are one-story mud structures, built low, so as to prevent any disastrous effects from earthquakes. The roofs are so flat and poorly constructed that during the rainy season a dry ceiling is rather the exception than the rule. Every building is covered with whitewash or white paint, and fronts directly on the street. There are plenty of back and side yards, but none in front. This is not so bad on the broad streets of a Russian town. In Tashkend they are exceptionally wide, with ditches on each side through which the water from the Tchirtchick ripples along beneath the double, and even quadruple, rows of poplars, acacias, and willows. These trees grow here with remarkable luxuriance, from a mere twig stuck into the ground. Although twenty years of Russian irrigation has given Nature a chance to rear thousands of trees on former barren wastes, yet wood is still comparatively scarce and dear.

The administration buildings of the city are for the most part exceedingly plain and unpretentious. In striking contrast is the new Russian cathedral, the recently erected school, and a large retail store built by a resident Greek, all of which are fine specimens of Russian architecture. Among its institutions are an observatory, a museum containing an embryo collection of Turkestan products and antiquities, and a medical dispensary for the natives, where vaccination is performed by graduates of medicine in the Tashkend school. The rather extensive library was originally collected for the chancellery of the governor-general, and contains the best collection of works on central Asia that is to be found in the world, including in its scope not only books and pamphlets, but even magazines and newspaper articles. For amusements, the city has a theater, a small imitation of the opera-house at Paris; and the Military Club, which, with its billiards and gambling, and weekly reunions, balls, and concerts, though a regular feature of a Russian garrison town, is especially pretentious in Tashkend. In size, architecture, and appointments, the club-house has no equal, we were told, outside the capital and Moscow.

Tashkend has long been known as a refuge for damaged reputations and shattered fortunes, or "the official purgatory following upon the emperor's displeasure." One of the finest houses of the city is occupied by the Grand Duke Nicholai Constantinovitch Romanoff, son of the late general admiral of the Russian navy, and first cousin to

PALACE OF THE CZAR'S NEPHEW, TASHKEND.

the Czar, who seems to be cheerfully resigned to his life in exile. Most of his time is occupied with the business of his silk-factory on the outskirts of Tashkend, and at his farm near Hodjent, which a certain firm in Chicago, at the time of our sojourn, was stocking with irrigating machinery. All of his bills are paid with checks drawn on his St. Petersburg trustees. His private life is rather unconventional and even democratic. Visitors to his household are particularly impressed with the beauty of his wife and the size of his liquor glasses. The example of the grand duke illustrates the sentiment in favor of industrial pursuits which is growing among the military classes, and even among the nobility, of Russia. The government itself, thanks to the severe lesson of the Crimean war, has learned that a great nation must stand upon a foundation of something more than aristocracy and nobility. To this influence is largely due the present growing prosperity of Tashkend, which, in military importance, is rapidly giving way to Askabad, "the key to Herat."

That spirit of equality and fraternity which characterizes the government of a Russian *mir*, or village, has been carried even into central Asia. We have frequently seen Russian peasants and natives occupying adjoining apartments in the same household, while in the process of trade all classes seem to fraternize in an easy and even cordial manner. The same is true of the children, who play together indiscriminately in the street. Many a one of these heterogeneous groups we have watched "playing marbles" with the ankle-bones of sheep, and listened, with some amusement, to their half Russian, half native jargon. Schools are now being established to educate the native children in the Russian language and methods, and native apprentices are being taken in by Russian merchants for the same purpose.

In Tashkend, as in every European city of the Orient, drunkenness, and gambling, and social laxity have followed upon the introduction of Western morals and culture. Jealousy and intrigue among the officers and functionaries are also not strange, perhaps, at so great a distance from headquarters, where the only avenue to distinction seems to lie through the public service. At the various dinner-parties and sociables given throughout the winter, the topic of war always met with general welcome. On one occasion a report was circulated that Abdurrahman Khan, the Ameer of Afghanistan, was lying at the point of death. Great preparations, it was said, were being made for an expedition over the Pamir, to establish on the throne

A SART RESCUING HIS CHILDREN FROM THE CAMERA OF THE "FOREIGN DEVILS."

the Russian candidate, Is-shah Khan from Samarkand, before Ayub Khan, the rival British protégé, could be brought from India. The young officers at once began to discuss their chances for promotion, and the number of decorations to be forthcoming from St. Petersburg. The social gatherings at Tashkend were more convivial than sociable. Acquaintances can eat and drink together with the greatest of good cheer, but there is very little sympathy in conversation. It was difficult for them to understand why we had come so far to see a country which to many of them was a place of exile.

An early spring did not mean an early departure from winter quarters. Impassable roads kept us anxious prisoners for a month and a half after the necessary papers had been secured. These included, in addition to the local passports, a carte-blanche permission to travel from Tashkend to Vladivostock through Turkestan and Siberia, a document obtained from St. Petersburg through the United States minister, the Hon. Charles Emory Smith. Of this route to the Pacific we were therefore certain, and yet, despite the universal opinion that a bicycle journey across the Celestial empire was impracticable, we had determined to continue on to the border line, and there to seek better information. "Don't go into China" were the last words of our many kind friends as we wheeled out of Tashkend on the seventh of May.

At Chimkend our course turned abruptly from what was once the main route between Russia's European and Asiatic capitals, and along which De Lesseps, in his letter to the Czar, proposed a line of railroad to connect Orenburg with Samarkand, a distance about equal to that between St. Petersburg and Odessa, 1483 miles. This is also the keystone in that wall of forts which Russia gradually raised around her unruly nomads of the steppes, and where, according to Gortchakoff's circular of 1864, "both interest and reason" required her to stop; and yet at that very time General Tchernaieff was advancing his forces upon the present capital, Tashkend. Here, too, we began that journey of 1500 miles along the Celestial mountain range which terminated only when we scaled its summit beyond Barkul to descend again into the burning sands of the Desert of Gobi. Here runs the great historical highway between China and the West.

From Auli-eta eastward we had before us about 200 miles of a vast steppe region. Near the mountains is a

VIEW OF CHIMKEND FROM THE CITADEL.

wilderness of lakes, swamps, and streams, which run dry in summer. This is the country of the "Thousand Springs" mentioned by the Chinese pilgrim Huen T'sang, and where was established the kingdom of Black China, supposed by many to have been one of the kingdoms of "Prester John." But far away to our left were the white sands of the Ak-Kum, over which the cloudless atmosphere quivers incessantly, like the blasts of a furnace. Of all these deserts, occupying probably one half of the whole Turkestan steppe, none is more terrible than that of the "Golodnaya Steppe," or Steppe of Hunger, to the north of the "White Sands" now before us. Even in the cool of evening, it is said that the soles of the wayfarer's feet become scorched, and the dog accompanying him finds no repose till he has burrowed below the burning surface. The monotonous appearance of the steppe itself is only intensified in winter, when the snow smooths over the broken surface, and even necessitates the placing of mud posts at regular intervals to mark the roadway for the Kirghiz post-drivers. But in the spring and autumn its arid surface is clothed, as if by enchantment, with verdure and prairie flowers. Both flowers and birds are gorgeously colored. One variety, about half the size of the jackdaw which infests the houses of Tashkend and Samarkand, has a bright blue body and red wings; another, resembling our field-lark in size and habits, combines a pink breast with black head and wings. But already this springtide splendor was beginning to disappear beneath the glare of approaching summer. The long wagon-trains of lumber, and the occasional traveler's tarantass rumbling along to the discord of its *duga* bells, were enveloped in a cloud of suffocating dust.

Now and then we would overtake a party of Russian peasants migrating from the famine-stricken districts of European Russia to the pioneer colonies along this Turkestan highway. The peculiarity of these villages is their extreme length, all the houses facing on the one wide street. Most of them are merely mud huts, others make pretensions to doors and windows, and a coat of whitewash. Near-by usually stands the old battered telega which served as a home during many months of travel over the Orenburg highway. It speaks well for the colonizing capacity of the Russians that they can be induced to come so many hundreds of miles from their native land, to settle in such a primitive way among the half-wild tribes of the steppes. As yet they do very little farming, but live, like the Kirghiz, by raising horses, cows, sheep, and goats, and, in addition, the Russian hog, the last resembling very much the wild swine of the jungles. Instead of the former military colonies of plundering Cossacks, who really become more assimilated to the Kirghiz than these to their conquerors, the *mir*, or communal system, is now penetrating these fertile districts, and systematically replacing the Mongolian culture. But the ignorance of this lower class of Russians is almost as noticeable as that of the natives themselves. As soon as we entered a village, the blacksmith left his anvil, the carpenter his bench, the storekeeper his counter, and the milkmaid her task. After our parade of the principal street, the crowd would gather round us at the station-house. All sorts of queries and ejaculations would pass among them. One would ask: "Are these gentlemen baptized? Are they really Christians?" On account of their extreme ignorance these Russian colonists are by no means able to cope with their German colleagues, who are given the poorest land, and yet make a better living.

The steppe is a good place for learning patience. With the absence of landmarks, you seem never to be getting anywhere. It presents the appearance of a boundless level expanse, the very undulations of which are so uniform as to conceal the intervening troughs. Into these, horsemen, and sometimes whole caravans, mysteriously disappear. In this way we were often enabled to surprise a herd of gazelles grazing by the roadside. They would stand for a moment with necks extended, and then scamper away like a shot, springing on their pipe-stem limbs three or four feet into the air. Our average rate was about seven miles an hour, although the roads were sometimes so soft with dust or sand as to necessitate the laying of straw for a foundation. There was scarcely an hour in the day when we were not accompanied by from one to twenty Kirghiz horsemen, galloping behind us with cries of "Yakshee!" ("Good!") They were especially curious to see how we crossed the roadside streams. Standing on the bank, they would watch intently every move as we stripped and waded through with bicycles and clothing on our shoulders. Then they would challenge us to a race, and, if the road permitted, we would endeavor to reveal some of the possibilities of the "devil's carts." On an occasion like this occurred one of our few mishaps. The road was lined by the occupants of a neighboring tent village, who had run out to see the race. One of the Kirghiz turned suddenly back in the opposite direction from which he had started. The wheel struck him at a rate of fifteen miles per hour, lifting him off his feet, and hurling over the handle-bars the rider, who fell upon his left arm, and twisted it out of place. With the assistance of the bystanders it was pulled back into the socket, and bandaged up till we reached the nearest Russian village. Here the only physician was an old blind woman of the faith-cure persuasion. Her massage treatment to replace the muscles was really effective, and was accompanied by prayers and by signs of the cross, a common method of

ON THE ROAD BETWEEN CHIMKEND AND VERNOYE.

treatment among the lower class of Russians. In one instance a cure was supposed to be effected by writing a prayer on a piece of buttered bread to be eaten by the patient.

Being users but not patrons of the Russian post-roads, we were not legally entitled to the conveniences of the post-stations. Tipping alone, as we found on our journey from Samarkand, was not always sufficient to preclude a request during the night to vacate the best quarters for the post-traveler, especially if he happened to wear the regulation brass button. To secure us against this inconvenience, and to gain some special attention, a letter was obtained from the overseer of the Turkestan post and telegraph district. This proved advantageous on many occasions, and once, at Auli-eta, was even necessary. We were surveyed with suspicious glances as soon as we entered the station-house, and when we asked for water to lave our hands and face, we were directed to the irrigating ditch in the street. Our request for a better room was answered by the question, if the one we had was not good enough, and how long we intended to occupy that. Evidently our English conversation had gained for us the covert reputation of being English spies, and this was verified in the minds of our hosts when we began to ask questions about the city prisons we had passed on our way. To every interrogation they replied, " I don't know." But presto, change, on the presentation of documents! Apologies were now profuse, and besides tea, bread, and eggs, the usual rations of a Russian post-station, we were exceptionally favored with chicken soup and *verainyik*, the latter consisting of cheese wrapped and boiled in dough, and then served in butter.

It has been the custom for travelers in Russia to decry the Russian post-station, but the fact is that an appreciation of this rather primitive form of accommodation depends entirely upon whether you approach it from a European hotel or from a Persian khan. Some are clean, while others are dirty. Nevertheless, it was always a welcome sight to see a small white building looming up in the dim horizon at the close of a long day's ride, and, on near approach, to observe the black and white striped post in front, and idle tarantasses around it. At the door would be found the usual crowd of Kirghiz post-drivers. After the presentation of documents to the *starosta*, who would hesitate at first about quartering our horses in the travelers' room, we would proceed at once to place our dust-covered heads beneath the spindle of the washing-tank. Although by this dripping-pan arrangement we would usually succeed in getting as much water down our backs as on our faces, yet we were consoled by the thought that too much was better than not enough, as had been the case in Turkey and Persia. Then we would settle down before the steaming samovar to meditate in solitude and quiet, while the rays of the declining sun shone on the gilded eikon in the corner of the room, and on the chromo-covered walls. When darkness fell, and the simmering music of the samovar had gradually died away; when the flitting swallows in the room had ceased their chirp, and settled down upon the rafters overhead, we ourselves would turn in under our fur-lined coats upon the leather-covered benches.

In consequence of the first of a series of accidents to our wheels, we were for several days the guests of the director of the botanical gardens at Pishpek. As a branch of the Crown botanical gardens at St. Petersburg, some valuable experiments were being made here with foreign seeds and plants. Peaches, we were told, do not thrive, but apples, pears, cherries, and the various kinds of berries, grow as well as they do at home. Rye, however, takes three years to reach the height of one year in America. Through the Russians, these people have obtained high-flown ideas of America and Americans. We saw

UPPER VALLEY OF THE CHU RIVER.

many chromos of American celebrities in the various station-houses, and the most numerous was that of Thomas A. Edison. His phonograph, we were told, had already made its appearance in Pishpek, but the natives did not seem to realize what it was. "Why," they said, "we have often heard better music than that." Dr. Tanner was not without his share of fame in this far-away country. During his fast in America, a similar, though not voluntary, feat was being performed here. A Kirghiz messenger who had been despatched into the mountains during the winter was lost in the snow, and remained for twenty-eight days without food. He was found at last, crazed by hunger. When asked what he would have to eat, he replied, "Everything." They foolishly gave him "everything," and in two days he was dead. For a long time he was called the "Doctor Tanner of Turkestan."

A divergence of seventy-five miles from the regular post-route was made in order to visit Lake Issik Kul, which is probably the largest lake for its elevation in the world, being about ten times larger than Lake Geneva, and at a height of 5300 feet. Its slightly brackish water, which never freezes, teems with several varieties of fish, many of which we helped to unhook from a Russian fisherman's line, and then helped to eat in his primitive hut near the shore. A Russian Cossack, who had just come over the snow-capped Ala Tau, "of the Shade," from Fort Narin, was also present, and from the frequent glances cast at the fisherman's daughter we soon discovered the object of his visit. The ascent to this lake, through the famous Buam Defile, or Happy Pass, afforded some of the grandest scenery on our route through Asia. Its seething, foaming, irresistible torrent needs only a large volume to make it the equal of the rapids at Niagara.

Our return to the post-road was made by an unbeaten track over the Ala Tau mountains. From the Chu valley, dotted here and there with Kirghiz tent villages and their grazing flocks and herds, we pushed our wheels up the broken path, which wound like a mythical stairway far up into the low-hanging clouds. We trudged up one of the steepest ascents we have ever made with a wheel. The scenery was grand, but lonely. The wild tulips, pinks, and verbenas dotting the green slopes furnished the only pleasant diversion from our arduous labor. Just as we turned the highest summit, the clouds shifted for a moment, and revealed before us two Kirghiz horsemen. They started back in astonishment, and gazed at us as though we were demons of the air, until we disappeared again down the opposite and more gradual slope. Late in the afternoon we emerged upon the plain, but no post-road or station-house was in sight, as we expected; nothing but a few Kirghiz kibitkas among the straggling rocks, like

KIRGHIZ ERECTING KIBITKAS BY THE CHU RIVER.

the tents of the Egyptian Arabs among the fallen stones of the pyramids.

Toward these we now directed our course, and, in view of a rapidly approaching storm, asked to purchase a night's lodging. This was only too willingly granted in anticipation of the coming *tomasha*, or exhibition. The milkmaids as they went out to the rows of sheep and goats tied to the lines of woolen rope, and the horsemen with reinless horses to drive in the ranging herds, spread the news from tent to tent. By the time darkness fell the kibitka was filled to overflowing. We were given the seat of honor opposite the doorway, bolstered up with blankets and pillows. By the light of the fire curling its smoke upward through the central opening in the roof, it was interesting to note the faces of our hosts. We had never met a people of a more peaceful temperament, and, on the other hand, none more easily frightened. A dread of the evil eye is one of their characteristics. We had not been settled long before the *ishan*, or itinerant dervish, was called in to drive away the evil spirits, which the "devil's carts" might possibly have brought. Immediately on entering, he began to shrug his shoulders, and to shiver as though passing into a state of trance. Our dervish acquaintance was a man of more than average intelligence. He had traveled in India, and had even heard some one speak of America. This fact alone was sufficient to warrant him in posing as instructor for the rest of the assembly. While we were drinking tea, a habit they have recently adopted from the Russians, he held forth at great length to his audience about the *Amerikón*.

The rain now began to descend in torrents. The felt covering was drawn over the central opening, and propped up at one end with a pole to emit the clouds of smoke from the smoldering fire. This was shifted with the veering wind. Although a mere circular rib framework covered with white or brown felt, according as the occupant is rich or poor, the Kirghiz kibitka, or more properly *yurt*, is not as a house builded upon the sand, even in the fiercest storm. Its stanchness and comfort are surprising when we consider the rapidity with which it may be taken down and transported. In half an hour a whole village may vanish, emigrating northward in summer, and southward in winter. Many a Kirghiz cavalcade was overtaken on the road, with long tent-ribs and felts tied upon the backs of two-humped camels, for the Bactrian dromedary has not been able to endure the severities of these Northern climates. The men would always be mounted on the camels' or horses' backs, while the women would be perched on the oxen and bullocks, trained for the saddle and as beasts of burden. The men never walk; if there is any leading to be done it falls to the women. The constant use of the saddle has made many of the men bandy-legged, which, in connection with their usual obesity,— with them a mark of dignity,— gives them a comical appearance.

After their curiosity regarding us had been partly satisfied, it was suggested that a sheep should be slaughtered in our honor. Neither meat nor bread is ever eaten by any but the rich Kirghiz. Their universal kumiss, corresponding to the Turkish yaourt, or coagulated milk, and other forms of lacteal dishes, sometimes mixed with meal, form the chief diet of the poor. The wife of our host, a buxom woman, who, as we had seen, could leap upon a horse's back as readily as a man, now entered the doorway, carrying a full-grown sheep by its woolly coat. This she twirled over on its back, and held down with her knee while the butcher artist drew a dagger from his belt, and held it aloft until the assembly stroked their scant beards, and uttered the solemn bismillah. Tired out by the day's ride, we fell asleep before the arrangements for the feast had been completed. When awakened near midnight, we found that the savory odor from the huge caldron on the fire had only increased the attraction and the crowd. The choicest bits were now selected for the guests. These consisted of pieces of liver, served with lumps of fat from the tail of their peculiarly fat-tailed sheep. As an act of the highest hospitality, our host dipped these into some liquid grease, and then, reaching over, placed them in our mouths with his fingers. It required considerable effort on this occasion to subject our feelings of nausea to a sense of Kirghiz politeness. In keeping with their characteristic generosity, every one in the kibitka must partake in some measure of the feast, although the women, who had done all the work, must be content with remnants and bones already picked over by the host. But this disposition to share everything was not without its other aspect; we also were expected to share everything with them. We were asked to bestow any little trinket or nicknack exposed to view. Any extra nut on the machine, a handkerchief, a packet of tea, or a lump of sugar, excited their cupidity at once. The latter was considered a bonbon by the women and younger portion of the spectators. The attractive daughter of our host, "Kumiss John," amused herself by stealing lumps of sugar from our pockets. When the feast was ended, the beards were again stroked, the name of Allah solemnly uttered by way of thanks for the bounty of heaven, and then each gave utterance to his appreciation of the meal.

Before retiring for the night, the dervish led the prayers, just as he had done at sunset. The praying-mats were spread, and all heads bowed toward Mecca. The only preparation for retiring was the spreading of blankets from the pile in one of the kibitkas. The Kirghiz are not in the habit of removing many garments for this purpose, and under the circumstances we found this custom a rather convenient one. Six of us turned in on the floor together, forming a semicircle, with our feet toward the fire. "Kumiss John," who was evidently the pet of the household, had a rudely constructed cot at the far end of the kibitka.

Vernoye, the old Almati, with its broad streets, low wood and brick houses, and Russian sign-boards, presented a Siberian aspect. The ruins of its many disastrous earth-

FANTASTIC RIDING AT THE SUMMER ENCAMPMENT OF THE COSSACKS.

quakes lying low on every hand told us at once the cause of its deserted thoroughfares. The terrible shocks of the year before our visit killed several hundred people, and a whole mountain in the vicinity sank. The only hope of its persistent residents is a branch from the Transsiberian or Transcaspian railroad, or the reannexation by Russia of the fertile province of Ili, to make it an indispensable depot. Despite these periodical calamities, Vernoye has had, and is now constructing, under the genius of the French architect, Paul L. Gourdet, some of the finest edifices to be found in central Asia. The orphan asylum, a magnificent three-story structure, is now being built on experimental lines, to test its strength against earthquake shocks.

One of the chief incidents of our pleasant sojourn was afforded by Governor Ivanoff. We were invited to head the procession of the Cossacks on their annual departure for their summer encampment in the mountains. After the usual religious ceremony, they filed out from the city parade-ground. Being unavoidably detained for a few moments, we did not come up until some time after the column had started. As we dashed by to the front with the American and Russian flags fluttering side by side from the handle-bars, cheer after cheer arose from the ranks, and even the governor and his party doffed their caps in acknowledgment. At the camp we were favored with a special exhibition of horsemanship. By a single twist of the rein the steeds would fall to the ground, and their riders crouch down behind them as a bulwark in battle. Then dashing forward at full speed, they would spring to the ground, and leap back again into the saddle, or, hanging by their legs, would reach over and pick up a handkerchief, cap, or a soldier supposed to be wounded. All these movements we photographed with our camera.

Of the endurance of these Cossacks and their Kirghiz horses we had a practical test. Overtaking a Cossack courier in the early part of a day's journey, he became so interested in the velocipede, as the Russians call the bicycle, that he determined to see as much of it as possible. He stayed with us the whole day, over a distance of fifty-five miles. His chief compensation was in witnessing the surprise of the natives to whom he would shout across the fields to come and see the *tomasha*, adding in explanation that we were the American gentlemen who had ridden all the way from America. Our speed was not slow, and frequently the poor fellow would have to resort to the whip, or shout, "Slowly, gentlemen, my horse is tired; the town is not far away, it is not necessary to hurry so." The fact is that in all our experience we found no horse of even the famed Kirghiz or Turkoman breed that could travel with the same ease and rapidity as ourselves even over the most ordinary road.

At Vernoye we began to glean practical information about China, but all except our genial host, M. Gourdet, counseled us against our proposed journey. He alone, as a traveler of experience, advised a divergence from the Siberan route at Altin Imell, in order to visit the Chinese city of Kuldja, where, as he said, with the assistance of the resident Russian consul we could test the validity of the Chinese passport received, as before mentioned, from the Chinese minister at London.

A few days later we were rolling up the valley of the Ili, having crossed that river by the well-constructed Russian bridge at Fort Iliysk, the head of navigation for the boats from Lake Balkash. New faces here met our curious gaze. As an ethnological transition between the inhabitants of central Asia and the Chinese, we were now among two distinctly agricultural races — the Dungans

STROLLING MUSICIANS.

and Taranchis. As the invited guests of these people on several occasions, we were struck with their extreme cleanliness, economy, and industry; but their deep-set eyes seem to express reckless cruelty.

The Mohammedan mosques of this people are like the Chinese pagodas in outward appearance, while they seem to be Chinese in half-Kirghiz garments. Their women, too, do not veil themselves, although they are much more shy than their rugged sisters of the steppes. Tenacious of their word, these people were also scrupulous about returning favors. Our exhibitions were usually rewarded by a spread of sweets and yellow Dungan tea. Of this we would partake beneath the shade of their well-trained grape-arbors, while listening to the music, or rather discord, of a peculiar stringed instrument played by the boys. Its bow of two parts was so interlaced with the strings of the instrument as to play upon two at every draw. Another musician usually accompanied by beating little sticks on a saucer.

These are the people who were introduced by the Manchus to replace the Kalmucks in the Kuldja district, and who in 1869 so terribly avenged upon their masters the blood they previously caused to flow. The fertile province of Kuldja, with a population of 2,500,000, was reduced by their massacres to one vast necropolis. On all sides are canals that have become swamps, abandoned fields, wasted forests, and towns and villages in ruins, in some of which the ground is still strewn with the bleached bones of the murdered.

As we ascended the Ili valley piles of stones marked in succession the sites of the towns of Turgen, Jarkend, Akkend, and Khorgos, names which the Russians are already reviving in their pioneer settlements. The largest of these, Jarkend, is the coming frontier town, to take the place of

THE CUSTOM-HOUSE AT KULDJA.

evacuated Kuldja. About twenty-two miles east of this point the large white Russian fort of Khorgos stands bristling on the bank of the river of that name, which, by the treaty of 1881, is now the boundary-line of the Celestial empire. On a ledge of rocks overlooking the ford a Russian sentinel was walking his beat in the solitude of a dreary outpost. He stopped to watch us as we plunged into the flood, with our Russian telega for a ferry-boat. "All 's well," we heard him cry, as, bumping over the rocky bottom, we passed from Russia into China. "Ah, yes," we thought; "'All 's well that ends well,' but this is only the beginning."

A few minutes later we dashed through the arched driveway of the Chinese custom-house, and were several yards away before the lounging officials realized what it was that flitted across their vision. "Stop! Come back!" they shouted in broken Russian. Amid a confusion of chattering voices, rustling gowns, clattering shoes, swinging pigtails, and clouds of opium and tobacco smoke, we were brought into the presence of the head official. Putting on his huge spectacles, he read aloud the visé written upon our American passports by the Chinese minister in London. His wonderment was increased when he further read that such a journey was being made on the "foot-moved carriages," which were being curiously fingered by the attendants. Our garments were minutely scrutinized, especially the buttons, while our caps and dark-colored spectacles were taken from our heads, and passed round for each to try on in turn, amid much laughter.

Owing to the predominant influence of Russia in these northwestern confines, our Russian papers would have been quite sufficient to cross the border into Kuldja. It was only beyond this point that our Chinese passport would be found necessary, and possibly invalid. After the usual

THE JOURNEY FROM SAMARKAND TO KULDJA 145

THE CHINESE MILITARY COMMANDER OF KULDJA.

visés had been stamped and written over, we were off on what proved to be our six months' experience in the "Middle Kingdom or Central Empire," as the natives call it, for to Chinamen there is a fifth point to the compass — the center, which is China. Not far on the road we heard the clatter of hoofs behind us. A Kalmuck was dashing toward us with a portentous look on his features. We dismounted in apprehension. He stopped short some twenty feet away, leaped to the ground, and, crawling up on hands and knees, began to *chin-chin* or knock his head on the ground before us. This he continued for some moments, and then without a word gazed at us in wild astonishment. Our perplexity over this performance was increased when, at a neighboring village, a bewildered

TWO CATHOLIC MISSIONARIES IN THE YARD OF OUR KULDJA INN.

Chinaman sprang out from the speechless crowd, and threw himself in the road before us. By a dexterous turn we missed his head, and passed over his extended queue.

Kuldja, with its Russian consul and Cossack station, still maintains a Russian telegraph and postal service. The mail is carried from the border in a train of three or four telegas, which rattle along over the primitive roads in a cloud of dust, with armed Cossacks galloping before and after, and a Russian flag carried by the herald in front. Even in the Kuldja post-office a heavily armed picket stands guard over the money-chest. This postal caravan we now overtook encamped by a small stream, during the glaring heat of the afternoon. We found that we had been expected several days before, and that quarters had been prepared for us in the postal station at the town of Suidun. Here we spent the night, and continued on to Kuldja the following morning.

Although built by the Chinese, who call it Nin-yuan, Kuldja, with its houses of beaten earth, strongly resembles the towns of Russian Turkestan. Since the evacuation by the Russians the Chinese have built around the city the usual quadrangular wall, thirty feet in height and twenty feet in width, with parapets still in the course of construction. But the rows of poplars, the whitewash, and the telegas were still left to remind us of the temporary Russian occupation. For several days we were objects of excited interest to the mixed population. The doors and windows of our Russian quarters were besieged by crowds. In defense of our host, we gave a public exhibition, and with the consent of the *Tootai* made the circuit on the top of the city walls. Fully 3000 people lined the streets and housetops to witness the race to which we had been challenged by four Dungan horsemen, riding below on the encircling roadway. The distance around was two miles. The horsemen started with a rush, and at the end of the first mile were ahead. At the third turning we overtook them, and came to the finish two hundred yards ahead, amid great excitement. Even the commander of the Kuldja forces was brushed aside by the chasing rabble.

A MORNING PROMENADE ON THE WALLS OF KULDJA.

V

OVER THE GOBI DESERT AND THROUGH THE WESTERN GATE OF THE GREAT WALL

RUSSIAN influence, which even now predominates at Kuldja, was forcibly indicated, the day after our arrival, during our investigations as to the validity of our Chinese passports for the journey to Peking. The Russian consul, whose favor we had secured in advance through letters from Governor Ivanoff at Vernoye, had pronounced them not only good, but by far the best that had been presented by any traveler entering China at this point. After endeavoring to dissuade us from what he called a foolhardy undertaking, even with the most valuable papers, he sent us, with his interpreter, to the Kuldja Tootai for the proper visé.

That dignitary, although deeply interested, was almost amused at the boldness of our enterprise. He said that no passport would insure success by the method we proposed to pursue; that, before he could allow us to make the venture, we must wait for an order from Peking. This, he said, would subject us to considerable delay and expense, even if the telegraph and post were utilized through Siberia and Kiakhta. This was discouraging indeed. But when we discovered, a few minutes later, that his highness had to call in the learned secretary to trace our proposed route for him on the map of China, and even to locate the capital, Peking, we began to question his knowledge of Chinese diplomacy. The matter was again referred to the consul, who reported back the following day that his previous assurances were reliable, that the Tootai would make the necessary visés, and send away at once, by the regular relay post across the empire, an open letter that could be read by the officials along the route, and be delivered long before our arrival at Peking. Such easy success we had not anticipated. The difficulty, as well as necessity, of obtaining the proper credentials for traveling in China was impressed upon us by the arrest the previous day of three Afghan visitors, and by the fact that a German traveler had been refused, just a few weeks before, permission even to cross the Mozart pass into Kashgar. So much, we thought, for Russian friendship.

Upon this assurance of at least official consent to hazard the journey to Peking, a telegram was sent to the chief of police at Tomsk, to whose care we had directed our letters, photographic material, and bicycle supplies to be sent from London in the expectation of being forced to take the Siberian route. These last could not have been dispensed with much longer, as our cushion-tires, ball-bearings, and axles were badly worn, while the rim of one of the rear wheels was broken in eight places for the lack of spokes. These supplies, however, did not reach us till six weeks after the date of our telegram, to which a prepaid reply was received, after a week's delay, asking in advance for the extra postage. This, with that prepaid from London, amounted to just fifty dollars. The warm weather, after the extreme cold of a Siberian winter, had caused the tires to stretch so much beyond their intended size that, on their arrival, they were almost unfit for use. Some of our photographic material also had been spoiled through the useless inspection of postal officials.

THE FORMER MILITARY COMMANDER OF KULDJA AND HIS FAMILY.

The delay thus caused was well utilized in familiarizing ourselves as much as possible with the language and characteristics of the Chinese, for, as we were without guides, interpreters, or servants, and in some places lacked even official assistance, no travelers, perhaps, were ever more dependent upon the people than ourselves. The Chinese language, the most primitive in the world, is, for this very reason perhaps, the hardest to learn. Its poverty of words reduces its grammar almost to a question of syntax and intonation. Many a time our expressions, by a wrong inflection, would convey a meaning different from the one intended. Even when told the difference, our ears could not detect it.

Our work of preparation was principally a process of elimination. We now had to prepare for a forced march in case of necessity. Handle-bars and seat-posts were shortened to save weight, and even the leather baggage-carriers, fitting in the frames of the machines, which we ourselves had patented before leaving England, were replaced by a couple of sleeping-bags made for us out of woolen shawls and Chinese oiled-canvas. The cutting off of buttons and extra parts of our clothing, as well as the shaving of our heads and faces, was also included by our friends in the list of curtailments. For the same reason one of our cameras, which we always carried on our backs, and refilled at night under the bedclothes, we sold to a Chinese photographer at Suidun, to make room for an extra provision-bag. The surplus film, with our extra baggage, was shipped by post, via Siberia and Kiakhta, to meet us on our arrival in Peking.

And now the money problem was the most perplexing of all. "This alone," said the Russian consul, "if nothing else, will defeat your plans." Those Western bankers who advertise to furnish "letters of credit to any part of the

VIEW OF A STREET IN KULDJA FROM THE WESTERN GATE.

world" are, to say the least, rather sweeping in their assertions. At any rate, our own London letter was of no use beyond the Bosporus, except with the Persian imperial banks run by an English syndicate. At the American Bible House at Constantinople we were allowed, as a personal favor, to buy drafts on the various missionaries along the route through Asiatic Turkey. But in central Asia we found that the Russian bankers and merchants would not handle English paper, and we were therefore compelled to send our letter of credit by mail to Moscow. Thither we had recently sent it on leaving Tashkend, with instructions to remit in currency to Irkutsk, Siberia. We now had to telegraph to that point to re-forward over the Kiakhta post-route to Peking. With the cash on hand, and the proceeds of the camera, sold for more than half its weight in silver, four and one third pounds, we thought we had sufficient money to carry us, or, rather, as much as we could carry, to that point; for the weight of the Chinese money necessary for a journey of over three thousand miles was, as the Russian consul thought, one of the greatest of our almost insurmountable obstacles. In the interior of China there is no coin except the *chen*, or *sapeks*, an alloy of copper and tin, in the form of a disk, having a hole in the center by which the coins may be strung together. The very recently coined *liang*, or *tael*, the Mexican piaster specially minted for the Chinese market, and the other foreign coins, have not yet penetrated from the coast. For six hundred miles over the border, however, we found both the Russian money and language serviceable among the Tatar merchants, while the *tenga*, or Kashgar silver-piece, was preferred by the natives even beyond the Gobi, being much handier than the larger or smaller bits of silver broken from the *yamba* bricks. All, however, would have to be weighed in the *tinza*, or small Chi-

OUR RUSSIAN FRIEND AND MR. SACHTLEBEN LOADED WITH ENOUGH CHINESE "CASH" TO PAY FOR A MEAL AT A KULDJA RESTAURANT.

nese scales we carried with us, and on which were marked the *fün, tchan,* and *liang* of the monetary scale. But the value of these terms is reckoned in *chen*, and changes with almost every district. This necessity for vigilance, together with the frequency of bad silver and loaded *yambas,* and the propensity of the Chinese to "knock down" on even the smallest purchase, tends to convert a traveler in China into a veritable Shylock. There being no banks or exchanges in the interior, we were obliged to purchase at Kuldja all the silver we would need for the entire journey of over three thousand miles. "How much would it take?" was the question that our past experience in Asiatic travel now aided us to answer. That our calculations were close is proved by the fact that we reached Peking with silver in our pockets to the value of half a dollar. Our money now constituted the principal part of our luggage, which, with camera and film, weighed just twenty-five pounds apiece. Most of the silver was chopped up into small bits, and placed in the hollow tubing of the machines to conceal it from Chinese inquisitiveness, if not something worse. We are glad to say, however, that no attempt at robbery was ever discovered, although efforts at extortion were frequent, and sometimes, as will appear, of a serious nature.

The blowing of the long horns and boom of the mortar cannon at the fort awoke us at daylight on the morning of July 13. Farewells had been said the night before. Only our good-hearted Russian host was up to put an extra morsel in our provision-bag, for, as he said, we could get no food until we reached the Kirghiz aouls on the high plateau of the Talki pass, by which we were to cut across over unbeaten paths to the regular so-called imperial highway, running from Suidun. From the Catholic missionaries at Kuldja we had obtained very accurate in-

A STREET IN THE TARANTCHI QUARTER OF KULDJA.

formation about this route as far as the Gobi desert. The expression Tian Shan Pe-lu, or northern Tian Shan route, in opposition to the Tian Shan Nan-lu, or southern Tian Shan route, shows that the Chinese had fully appreciated the importance of this historic highway, which continues the road running from the extreme western gate of the Great Wall obliquely across Mongolian Kan-su, through Hami and Barkul, to Urumtsi. From here the two natural highways lead, one to the head-waters of the Black Irtish, the other to the passes leading into the Ili valley, and other routes of the Arolo-Caspian depression. The latter route, which is now commanded at intervals by Chinese forts and military settlements, was recently relinquished by Russia only when she had obtained a more permanent footing on the former in the trading-posts of Chuguchak and Kobdo, for she very early recognized the importance of this most natural entry to the only feasible route across the Chinese empire. In a glowing sunset, at the end of a hot day's climb, we looked for the last time over the Ili valley, and at dusk, an hour later, rolled into one of the Kirghiz aouls that are here scattered among the rich pasturage of the plateau.

Even here we found that our reputation had extended from Kuldja. The chief advanced with *amans* of welcome, and the heavy-matted curtains in the kibitka doorway were raised, as we passed, in token of honor. When the refreshing kumiss was served around the evening campfire, the dangers of the journey through China were discussed among our hosts with frequent looks of misgiving. Thus, from first to last, every judgment was against us, and every prediction was of failure, if not of something worse; and now, as we stole out from the tent by the light of the rising moon, even the specter-like mountain-peaks around us, like symbols of coming events, were casting their shadows before. There was something so illusive in the scene as to make it very impressive. In the morning, early, a score of horsemen were ready to escort us on the road. At parting they all dismounted and uttered a prayer to Allah for our safety; and then as we rode away, drew their fingers across their throats in silence, and waved a solemn good-by. Such was the almost superstitious fear of these western nomads for the land which once sent forth a Yengiz Khan along this very highway.

Down the narrow valley of the Kuitun, which flows into

PRACTISING OUR CHINESE ON A KULDJA CULPRIT.

the Ebi-nor, startling the mountain deer from the brink of the tree-arched rivulet, we reached a spot which once was the haunt of a band of those border-robbers about

THE HEAD OF A BRIGAND EXPOSED ON THE HIGHWAY.

whom we had heard so much from our apprehensive friends. At the base of a volcano-shaped mountain lay the ruins of their former dens, from which only a year ago they were wont to sally forth on the passing caravans. When they were exterminated by the government, the head of their chief, with its dangling queue, was mounted on a pole near-by, and preserved in a cage from birds of prey, as a warning to all others who might aspire to the same notoriety. In this lonely spot we were forced to spend the night, as here occurred, through the carelessness of the Kuldja Russian blacksmith, a very serious break in one of our gear wheels. It was too late in the day to walk back the sixteen miles to the Kirghiz encampment, and there obtain horses for the remaining fifty-eight miles to Kuldja, for nowhere else, we concluded, could such a break be mended. Our sleeping-bags were now put to a severe test between the damp ground and the heavy mountain dew. The penetrating cold, and the occasional panther-like cry of some prowling animal, kept us awake the greater part of the night, awaiting with revolvers in hand some expected attack.

Five days later we had repassed this spot and were toiling over the sand and saline-covered depression of the great "Han-Hai," or Dried-up Sea. The mountain freshets, dissolving the salt from their sandy channels, carry it down in solution and deposit it with evaporation in massive layers, forming a comparatively hard roadway in the midst of the shifting sand-dunes. Over these latter our progress was extremely slow. One stretch of fifteen miles, which it took us six hours to cover, was as formidable as any part of the Turkoman desert along the Transcaspian railway. At an altitude of only six hundred feet above the sea, according to our aneroid barometer, and beneath the rays of a July sun against which even our felt caps were not much protection, we were half-dragging, half-pushing, our wheels through a foot of sand, and slapping at the mosquitos swarming upon our necks and faces. These pests, which throughout this low country are the largest and most numerous we have ever met, are bred in the intermediate swamps, which exist only through the negligence of the neighboring villagers. At night smoldering fires, which half suffocate the human inmates, are built before the doors and windows to keep out the intruding insects. All travelers wear gloves, and a huge hood covering the head and face up to the eyes, and in their hands carry a horse-tail switch to lash back and forth over their shoulders. Being without such protection we suffered both day and night.

A CHINESE GRAVEYARD ON THE EASTERN OUTSKIRTS OF KULDJA.

The mountain freshets all along the road to Urumtsi were more frequent and dangerous than any we had yet encountered. Toward evening the melting snows, and the condensing currents from the plain heated during the day, fill and overflow the channels that in the morning are almost dry. One stream, with its ten branches, swept the stones and boulders over a shifting channel one mile in width. It was when wading through such streams as this, where every effort was required to balance ourselves and our luggage, that the mosquitos would make up for lost time with impunity. The river, before reaching Manas, was so swift and deep as to necessitate the use of regular government carts. A team of three horses, on making a misstep, were shifted away from the ford into deep water and carried far down the stream. A caravan of Chinese traveling-vans, loaded with goods from India, were crossing at the time, on their way to the outlying provinces and the Russian border. General Bauman at Vernoye had informed us that in this way English goods were swung clear around the circle and brought into Russia through the unguarded back door.

With constant wading and tramping, our Russian shoes and stockings, one of which was almost torn off by the sly grab of a Chinese spaniel, were no longer fit for use. In their place we were now obliged to purchase the short, white cloth Chinese socks and string sandals, which for mere cycling purposes and wading streams proved an excellent substitute, being light and soft on the feet and very quickly dried. The calves of our legs, however, being left bare, we were obliged, for state occasions at least, to retain and utilize the upper portion of our old stockings. It was owing to this scantiness of wardrobe that we were obliged when taking a bath by the roadside streams to make a quick wash of our linen, and put it on wet to

SPLITTING POPPY-HEADS TO START THE OPIUM JUICE.

dry, or allow it to flutter from the handle-bars as we rode along. It was astonishing even to ourselves how little a man required when once beyond the pale of Western conventionalities.

From Manas to Urumtsi we began to strike more tillage and fertility. Maize, wheat, and rice were growing, but rather low and thin. The last is by no means the staple food of China, as is commonly supposed, except in the southern portion. In the northern, and especially the outlying, provinces it is considered more a luxury for the wealthy. Millet and coarse flour, from which the *mien* or dough-strings are made, is the foundation, at least, for more than half the subsistence of the common classes. Nor is there much truth, we think, in the assertion that Chinamen eat rats, although we sometimes regretted that they did not. After a month or more without meat a dish of rats would have been relished, had we been able to get it. On the other hand we have learned that there is a society of Chinamen who are vegetarians from choice, and still another that will eat the meat of no animal, such as the ass, horse, dog, etc., which can serve man in a better way.

Urumtsi, or Hun-miao (red temple) of the Chinese, still retains its ancient prestige in being the seat of government for the viceroyalty of Sin-tsiang, which includes all that portion of western China lying without the limit of Mongolia and Tibet. Thanks to its happy position, it has always rapidly recovered after every fresh disaster. It now does considerable trade with Russia through the town of Chuguchak, and with China through the great gap which here occurs in the Tian Shan range. It lies in a picturesque amphitheater behind the solitary "Holy Mount," which towers above a well-constructed bridge across its swiftly flowing river. This city was one of our principal

THE CHIEF OF THE CUSTOM-HOUSE GIVES A LESSON IN OPIUM SMOKING.

168   ACROSS ASIA ON A BICYCLE

landmarks across the empire; a long stage of the journey was here completed.

On entering a Chinese city we always made it a rule to run rapidly through until we came to an inn, and then lock up our wheels before the crowd could collect. Urumtsi, however, was too large and intricate for such a manœuver.

RIDING BEFORE THE GOVERNOR OF MANAS.

We were obliged to dismount in the principal thoroughfare. The excited throng pressed in upon us. Among them was a Chinaman who could talk a little Russian, and who undertook to direct us to a comfortable inn at the far end of the city. This street parade gathered to the inn yard an overwhelming mob, and announced to the whole community that "the foreign horses" had come. It had been posted, we were told, a month before, that "two people of the new world" were coming through on "strange iron horses," and every one was requested not to molest them. By this, public curiosity was raised to the highest pitch. When we returned from supper at a neighboring restaurant, we were treated to a novel scene. The doors and windows of our apartments had been blocked with boxes, bales of cotton, and huge cart-wheels to keep out the irrepressible throng. Our host was agitated to tears; he came out wringing his hands, and urging upon us that any attempt on our part to enter would cause a rush that would break his house down. We listened to his entreaties on the condition that we should be allowed to mount to the roof with a ladder, to get away from the annoying curiosity of the crowd. There we sat through the evening twilight, while the crowd below, somewhat balked, but not discouraged, stood taking in every move. Nightfall and a drizzling rain came at last to our relief.

The next morning a squad of soldiers was despatched to raise the siege, and at the same time presents began to arrive from the various officials, from the Tsongtu, or viceroy, down to the superintendent of the local prisons. The matter of how much to accept of a Chinese present, and how much to pay for it, in the way of a tip to the bearer, is one of the finest points of that finest of fine arts, Chinese etiquette; and yet in the midst of such an abundance and variety we were hopelessly at sea. Fruits and teas were brought, together with meats and chickens, and even a live sheep. Our Chinese visiting-cards—with the Chinese the great insignia of rank—were now returned for those sent with the presents, and the hour appointed for the exhibition of our bicycles as requested.

Long before the time, the streets and housetops leading from the inn to the viceroy's palace at the far end of the city began to fill with people, and soldiers were detailed at our request to make an opening for us to ride through abreast. This, however, did not prevent the crowd from pushing us against each other, or sticking sticks in the wheels, or throwing their hats and shoes in front of us, as we rode by. When in sight of the viceroy's palace, they closed in on us entirely. It was the worst jam we had ever been in. By no possibility could we mount our machines, although the mob was growing more and more impatient. They kept shouting for us to ride, but would give us no room. Those on the outside pushed the inner ones against us. With the greatest difficulty could we preserve our equilibrium, and prevent the wheels from being crushed, as we surged along toward the palace gate; while all the time our Russian interpreter, Mafoo, on horseback in front, continued to shout and gesticulate in the wildest manner above their heads. Twenty soldiers had been stationed at the palace gate to keep back the mob

MONUMENT TO A PRIEST AT URUMTSI.

with cudgels. When we reached them, they pulled us and our wheels quickly through into the inclosure, and then tried to stem the tide by belaboring the heads and shoulders in reach, including those of our unfortunate interpreter, Mafoo. But it was no use. Everything was swept away before this surging wave of humanity. The

A BANK IN URUMTSI.

viceroy himself, who now came out to receive us, was powerless. All he could do was to request them to make room around the palace courtyard for the coming exhibition. Thousands of thumbs were uplifted that afternoon, in praise of the wonderful *twee-tah-cheh*, or two-wheeled carts, as they witnessed our modest attempt at trick riding and special manœuvering. After refreshments in the palace, to which we were invited by the viceroy, we were counseled to leave by a rear door, and return by a roundabout way to the inn, leaving the mob to wait till dark for our exit from the front.

The restaurant or tea-house in China takes the place of the Western club-room. All the current news and gossip is here circulated and discussed over their eating or gambling. One of their games of chance, which we have frequently noticed, seems to consist in throwing their fingers at one another, and shouting at the top of their voices. It is really a matching of numbers, for which the Chinamen make signs on their fingers, up to the numeral ten. Our entry into a crowded *dungan,* or native Mohammedan restaurant, the next morning, was the signal for exciting accounts of the events of the previous day. We were immediately invited to take tea with this one, a morning dish of *tung-posas,* or nut and sugar dumplings, with another, while a third came over with his can of *sojeu,* or Chinese gin, with an invitation "to join him." The Chinese of all nations seem to live in order to eat, and from this race of epicures has developed a nation of excellent cooks. Our fare in China, outside the Gobi district, was far better than in Turkey or Persia, and, for this reason, we were better able to endure the increased hardships. A plate of sliced meat stewed with vegetables, and served with a piquant sauce, sliced radishes and onions with vinegar, two loaves of Chinese *mo-mo,* or steamed bread, and a pot of tea, would usually cost us about three and one quarter cents apiece. Everything in China is sliced so that it can be eaten with the chop-sticks. These we at length learned to manipulate with sufficient dexterity to pick up a dove's egg — the highest attainment in the chop-stick art. The Chinese have rather a sour than a sweet tooth. Sugar is rarely used in anything, and never in tea. The steeped tea-flowers, which the higher classes use, are really more tasty without it. In many of the smaller towns, our visits to the restaurant would sometimes result in considerable damage to its keepers, for the crowd would swarm in after us, knocking over the table, stools, and crockery as they went, and collect in a circle around us to watch the "foreigners" eat, and to add their opium and tobacco smoke to the suffocating atmosphere.

A visit to the local mint in Urumtsi revealed to us the primitive method of making the *chen*, or money-disks before mentioned. Each is molded instead of cut and stamped as in the West. By its superintendent we were

A MAID OF WESTERN CHINA.

invited to a special breakfast on the morning of our departure.

The Chinese are the only people in the Orient, and, so far as we know, in the European and Asiatic continents, who resemble the Americans in their love for a good, substantial morning meal. This was much better adapted to our purpose than the Russian custom, which compelled us to do the greater part of our day's work on merely bread and weak tea.

STYLISH CART OF A CHINESE MANDARIN.

From Urumtsi we had decided to take the northern route to Hami, via Gutchen and Barkul, in order to avoid as much as possible the sands of the Tarim basin on the southern slope of the Tian Shan mountains. Two guards were commissioned by the viceroy to take us in charge, and hand us over to the next relay station. Papers were given them to be signed by the succeeding authorities on our safe arrival. This plan had been adopted by every chief mandarin along the route, in order, not only to follow out the request of the London minister as written on the passport, but principally to do us honor in return for the favor of a bicycle exhibition; but many times we would leave our discomfited guards to return with unsigned papers. Had we been traveling in the ordinary way, not only these favors might not have been shown us, but our project entirely defeated by local obstructions, as was the case with many who attempted the same journey by caravan. To the good-will of the mandarins, as well as the people, an indispensable concomitant of a journey through China, our bicycles were after all our best passports. They everywhere overcame the antipathy for the foreigner, and made us cordially welcome.

The costumes of our soldiers were strikingly picturesque. Over the front and back of the scarlet waistcoats were worked in black silk letters their military credentials. Over their full baggy trousers were drawn their riding overalls, which cover only the front and sides of the legs, the back being cut out just above the cloth top of their Chinese boots. Instead of a cap, they wear a piece of printed cloth wrapped tightly around the head, like the American washerwomen. Their well-cushioned saddles did not save them from the constant jolting to which our high speed subjected them. At every stopping-place they would hold forth at length to the curious crowd about their roadside experiences. It was amusing to hear their graphic descriptions of the mysterious "ding," by which they referred to the ring of the cyclometer at every mile. But the phrase *quai-ti-henn* (very fast), which concluded almost every sentence, showed what feature impressed them most. Then, too, they disliked very much to travel in the heat of the day, for all summer traveling in China

A CHINESE PEDDLER FROM BARKUL.

is done at night. They would wake us up many hours before daylight to make a start, despite our previous request to be left alone. Our week's run to Barkul was made, with a good natural road and favoring conditions, at the rate of fifty-three miles per day, eight miles more than our general average across the empire. From Kuldja to the Great Wall, where our cyclometer broke, we took accurate measurements of the distances. In this way, we soon discovered that the length of a Chinese *li* was even more changeable than the value of the *tael*. According to time and place, from 185 to 250 were variously reckoned to a degree, while even a difference in direction would very often make a considerable difference in the distance. It is needless to say that, at this rate, the guards did not stay with us. Official courtesy was now confined to despatches sent in advance. Through this exceptionally wild district were encountered several herds of antelope and wild asses, which the natives were hunting with their long, heavy, fork-resting rifles. Through the exceptional tameness of the jack-rabbits along the road, we were sometimes enabled to procure with a revolver the luxury of a meat supper.

At Barkul (Tatar) the first evidence of English influence began to appear in the place of the fading Russian, although the traces of Russian manufacture were by no means wanting far beyond the Great Wall. English pulverized sugar now began to take the place of Russian lump. India rubber, instead of the Russianized French *elastique*, was the native name for our rubber tires. English letters, too, could be recognized on the second-hand paper and bagging appropriated to the natives' use, and even the gilded buttons worn by the soldiers bore the stamp of "treble gilt." From here the road to Hami turns abruptly south, and by a pass of over nine thousand feet crosses the declining spurs of the Tian Shan mountains, which stand like a barrier between the two great historic highways, deflecting the westward waves of migration, some to Kashgaria and others to Zungaria. On the southern slope of the pass we met with many large caravans of donkeys, dragging down pine-logs to serve as poles in the proposed extension of the telegraph-line from Su-Chou to Urumtsi. In June of this year the following item appeared in the newspapers:

"Within a few months Peking will be united by wire with St. Petersburg; and, in consequence, with the telegraph system of the entire civilized world. According to the latest issue of the Turkestan 'Gazette,' the tele-

CHINESE GRAVES ON THE ROAD TO HAMI.

graph-line from Peking has been brought as far west as the city of Kashgar. The European end of the line is at Osh, and a small stretch of about 140 miles now alone breaks the direct telegraph communication from the Atlantic to the Pacific."

Hami is one of those cities which may be regarded as indispensable. At the edge of the Great Gobi and the converging point of the Nan-lu and Pe-lu—that is, the southern and northern routes to the western world—this oasis is a necessary resting-place. During our stop of two days, to make necessary repairs and recuperate our strength for the hardships of the desert, the usual calls were exchanged with the leading officials. In the matter of social politeness the Chinese, especially the "literati," have reason to look down upon the barbarians of the West. Politeness has been likened generally to an air-cushion. There is nothing in it, but it eases the jolts wonderfully. As a mere ritual of technicalities it has perhaps reached its highest point in China. The multitude of honorific titles, so bewildering and even maddening to the Occidental, are here used simply to keep in view the fixed relations of graduated superiority. When wishing to be exceptionally courteous to "the foreigners," the more experienced mandarins would lay their doubled fists in the palms of our hands, instead of raising them in front of their foreheads, with the usual salutation *Homa*. In shaking hands with a Chinaman we thus very often had our hands full. After the exchange of visiting-cards, as an

SCENE IN A TOWN OF WESTERN CHINA.

indication that their visits would be welcome, they would come on foot, in carts, or palanquins, according to their rank, and always attended by a larger or smaller retinue.

Our return visits would always be made by request, on the wheels, either alone or with our interpreter, if we could find one, for our Chinese was as yet painfully defective. Russian had served us in good stead, though not always

A LESSON IN CHINESE.

directly. In a conversation with the Tootai of Schicho, for instance, our Russian had to be translated into Turki and thence interpreted in Chinese. The more intelligent of these conversations were about our own and other countries of the world, especially England and Russia, who, it was rumored, had gone to war on the Afghanistan border. But the most of them generally consisted of a series of trivial interrogations beginning usually with:

THE GOBI DESERT AND THE GREAT WALL 181

"How old are you?" Owing to our beards, which were now full grown, and which had gained for us the frequent title of *yeh renn*, or wild men, the guesses were far above the mark. One was even as high as sixty years, for the reason, as was stated, that no Chinaman could raise such a beard before that age. We were frequently surprised at their persistence in calling us brothers when there was no apparent reason for it, and were finally told that we must be " because we were both named *Mister* on our passports."

It was already dusk on the evening of August 10 when we drew up to the hamlet of Shang-loo-shwee at the end of the Hami oasis. The Great Gobi, in its awful loneliness, stretched out before us, like a vast ocean of endless space. The growing darkness threw its mantle on the scene, and left imagination to picture for us the nightmare of our boyhood days. We seemed, as it were, to be standing at the end of the world, looking out into the realm of nowhere. Foreboding thoughts disturbed our repose, as we contemplated the four hundred miles of this barren stretch to the Great Wall of China. With an early morning start, however, we struck out at once over the eighty-five miles of the Takla Makan sands. This was the worst we could have, for beyond the caravan station of Kooshee we would strike the projecting limits of Mongolian Kan-su. This narrow tract, now lying to our left between Hami and the Nan Shan mountains, is characterized by considerable diversity in its surface, soil, and climate. Traversed by several copious streams from the Nan Shan mountains, and the moisture-laden currents from the Bay of Bengal and the Brahmaputra valley, its "desert" stretches are not the dismal solitudes of the Tarim basin or the "Black" and "Red" sands of central Asia. Water is found almost everywhere near the sur-

12*

face, and springs bubble up in the hollows, often encircled by exterior oases. Everywhere the ground is traversable by horses and carts. This comparatively fertile tract, cutting the Gobi into two great sections, has been, ever since its conquest two thousand years ago, of vast importance to China, being the only feasible avenue of commu-

A TRAIL IN THE GOBI DESERT.

nication with the western provinces, and the more important link in the only great highway across the empire. A regular line of caravan stations is maintained by the constant traffic both in winter and summer. But we were now on a bit of the genuine Gobi—that is, "Sandy Desert"—of the Mongolian, or "Shamo" of the Chinese. Everywhere was the same interminable picture of vast undulating plains of shifting reddish sands, interspersed with quartz pebbles, agates, and carnelians, and relieved here and there by patches of wiry shrubs, used as fuel at the desert stations, or lines of hillocks succeeding each other like waves on the surface of the shoreless deep. The wind, even more than the natural barrenness of the soil, prevents the growth of any vegetation except low, pliant herbage. Withered plants are uprooted and scattered by the gale like patches of foam on the stormy sea. These terrible winds, which of course were against us, with the frequently heavy cart-tracks, would make it quite impossible to ride. The monotony of many weary hours of plodding was relieved only by the bones of some abandoned beast of burden, or the occasional train of Chinese carts, or rather two-wheeled vans, loaded with merchandise, and drawn by five to six horses or mules. For miles away they would see us coming, and crane their necks in wondering gaze as we approached. The mulish leaders, with distended ears, would view our strange-looking vehicles with suspicion, and then lurch far out in their twenty-

IN THE GOBI DESERT.

foot traces, pulling the heavily loaded vehicles from the deep-rutted track. But the drivers were too busy with their eyes to notice any little divergence of this kind. Dumb with astonishment they continued to watch us till we disappeared again toward the opposite horizon. Farther on we would meet a party of Chinese emigrants or exiles, on their way to the fertile regions that skirt the northern and southern slopes of the Tian Shan mountains. By these people even the distant valley of the Ili is being largely populated. Being on foot, with their extraordinary loads balanced on flexible shoulder-poles, these poor fellows could make only one station, or from twelve to twenty miles a day. In the presence of their patience and endurance, we were ashamed to think of such a thing as hardship.

The station-houses on the desert were nothing more than a collection of mud huts near a surface well of strongly brackish water. Here, most of the caravans would put up during the day, and travel at night. There was no such thing as a restaurant; each one by turn must do his own cooking in the inn kitchen, open to all. We, of course, were expected to carry our own provisions and do our own culinary work like any other respectable travelers. This we had frequently done before where restaurants were not to be found. Many a time we would enter an inn with our arms filled with provisions, purchased at the neighboring bazaars, take possession of the oven and cooking utensils, and proceed to get up an American meal, while all the time a hundred eyes or more would be staring at us in blank amazement. But here on the desert we could buy nothing but very coarse flour. When asked if they had an egg or a piece of vegetable, they would shout "*Ma-you*" ("There is none") in a tone of rebuke, as much as to say: "My conscience! man, what do you expect on the Gobi?" We would have to be content with our own tea made in the iron pot, fitting in the top of the mud oven, and a kind of sweetened bread made up with our supply of sugar brought from Hami. This we nicknamed our "Gobi cake," although it did taste rather strongly of brackish water and the garlic of previous contents of the one common cooking-pot. We would usually take a large supply for road use on the following day, or, as sometimes proved, for the midnight meal of the half-starved inn-dog. The interim between the evening meal and bedtime was always employed in writing notes by the

STATION OF SEB-BOO-TCHAN.

feeble, flickering light of a primitive taper-lamp, which was the best we had throughout the Chinese journey.

A description of traveling in China would by no means be complete without some mention of the vermin which infest, not only inns and houses, but the persons of nearly all the lower classes. Lice and fleas seem to be the *sine qua non* of Chinese life, and in fact the itching with some seems to furnish the only occasion for exercise. We have seen even shopkeepers before their doors on a sunny afternoon, amusing themselves by picking these insidious creatures from their inner garments. They are one of the necessary evils it seems, and no secret is made of it. The sleeping *kangs* of the Chinese inns, which are made of beaten earth and heated in winter like an oven, harbor these pests the year round, not to mention the filthy coverlets and greasy pillows that were sometimes offered us. Had we not had our own sleeping-bags, and used the camera, provision-bag, and coats for pillows, our life would have been intolerable. As it was there was but little rest for the weary.

The longest station on the desert was thirty-one miles. This was the only time that we suffered at all with thirst. In addition to the high mean elevation of the Gobi, about four thousand feet, we had cloudy weather for a considerable portion of the journey, and, in the Kan-su district, even a heavy thunder-shower. These occasional summer rains form, here and there, temporary meres and lakes, which are soon evaporated, leaving nothing behind except a saline efflorescence. Elsewhere the ground is furrowed by sudden torrents tearing down the slopes of the occasional hills or mountains. These dried up river-beds furnished the only continuously hard surfaces we found on the Gobi; although even here we were sometimes brought up with a round turn in a chuck hole, with the sand flying above our heads.

Our aneroid barometer registered approximately six thousand five hundred feet, when we reached at dusk the summit of the highest range of hills we encountered on the desert journey. But instead of the station-hut we expected to find, we were confronted by an old Mongolian monastery. These institutions, we had found, were generally situated as this one, at the top of some difficult mountain-pass or at the mouth of some cavernous gorge, where the pious intercessors might, to the best advantage, strive to appease the wrathful forces of nature. In this line of duty the lama was no doubt engaged when we walked into his feebly-lighted room, but, like all Orientals, he would let nothing interfere with the performance of his religious duties. With his gaze centered upon one spot, his fingers flew over the string of beads in his lap,

A ROCKY PASS IN THE MOUNTAINS OF THE GOBI.

and his tongue over the stereotyped prayers, with a rapidity that made our head swim. We stood unnoticed till the end, when we were at once invited to a cup of tea, and directed to our destination, five *li* beyond. Toward this we plodded through the growing darkness and rapidly cooling atmosphere; for in its extremes of temperature the Gobi is at once both Siberian and Indian, and that, too, within the short period of a few hours. Some of the mornings of what proved to be very hot days were cold enough to make our extremities fairly tingle.

A constant diet of bread and tea, together with the

hard physical exercise and mental anxiety, caused our strength at length to fail.

The constant drinking of brackish water made one of us so ill that he could retain no food. A high fever set in on the evening of August 15, and as we pulled into the station of Bay-doon-sah, he was forced to go to bed at once. The other, with the aid of our small medicine supply, endeavored to ward off the ominous symptoms. In his anxiety, however, to do all that was possible he made a serious blunder. Instead of antipyrin he administered the poison, sulphate of zinc, which we carried to relieve our eyes when inflamed by the alkali dust. This was swallowed before the truth was discovered. It was

A WASTE OF BLACK SAND IN THE GOBI.

an anxious moment for us both when we picked up the paper from the floor and read the inscription. We could do nothing but look at each other in silence. Happily it was an overdose, and the vomiting which immediately followed relieved both the patient and the anxious doctor. What to do we did not know. The patient now suggested that his companion should go on without him, and, if possible, send back medical aid or proper food; but not to remain and get worse himself. He, on the other hand,

A ROAD MARK IN THE GOBI DESERT.

refused to leave without the other. Then too, the outlying town of Ngan-si-chou, the first where proper food and water could be obtained, was only one day's journey away. Another effort was decided upon. But when morning came, a violent hurricane from the southeast swept the sand in our faces, and fairly blew the sick man over on his wheel. Famishing with thirst, tired beyond expression, and burning with fever as well as the withering heat, we reached at last the bank of the Su-la-ho. Eagerly we plunged into its sluggish waters, and waded through under the walls of Ngan-si-chou.

Ngan-si-chou was almost completely destroyed during the late Dungan rebellion. Little is now to be seen except heaps of rubbish, ruined temples, and the scattered fragments of idols. The neglected gardens no longer check the advancing sands, which in some places were drifting over the ramparts. Through its abandoned gateway we almost staggered with weakness, and directed our course to the miserable bazaar. The only meat we could find was pork, that shibboleth between Mohammedanism and Confucianism. The Dungan restaurant-keeper would not cook it, and only after much persuasion consented to have it prepared outside and brought back to be eaten beneath his roof. With better water and more substantial food we began, from this time on, to recuperate. But before us still a strong head wind was sweeping over the many desert stretches that lay between the oases along the Su-la-ho, and with the constant walking our sandals and socks were almost worn away. For this reason we were delayed one evening in reaching the town of Dyou-min-shan. In the lonely stillness of its twilight a horseman was approaching across the barren plain, bearing a huge Chinese lantern in his hand, and singing aloud, as is a Chinaman's custom, to drive off the evil spirits of the night. He started back, as we suddenly appeared, and then dismounted, hurriedly, to throw his lantern's glare upon us. "Are you the two Americans?" he asked in an agitated manner. His question was surprising. Out in this desert country we were not aware that our identity was known, or our visit expected. He then explained that he had been instructed by the magistrate of Dyou-min-shan to go out and look for us, and escort us into the town. He also mentioned in this connection the name of Ling Darin — a name that we had heard spoken of almost with veneration ever since leaving Urumtsi. Who this personage was we were unable to find out beyond that he was an influential mandarin in the city of Su-chou, now only a day's journey away.

Near that same fortieth parallel of latitude on which

our Asiatic journey was begun and ended, we now struck, at its extreme western limit, the Great Wall of China. The Kiayu-kuan, or "Jade Gate," by which it is here intersected, was originally so called from the fact that it led into the Khotan country, whence the Chinese traders brought back the precious mineral. This, with the Shang-

WITHIN THE WESTERN GATE OF THE GREAT WALL.

hai-kuan near the sea, and the Yuamin-kuan, on the Nankow pass, are the principal gateways in this "wall of ten thousand *li*," which, until forced by Yengiz Khan, protected the empire from the Mongolian nomads for a period of fourteen hundred years. In its present condition the Great Wall belongs to various epochs. With the sudden and violent transitions of temperature in the severe Mongolian climate, it may be doubted whether any portion of Shi Hoangti's original work still survives. Nearly all the eastern section, from Ordos to the Yellow Sea, was rebuilt in the fifth century, and the double rampart along the northwest frontier of the plains of Peking was twice restored in the fifteenth and sixteenth. North of Peking, where this prodigious structure has a mean height of about twenty-six feet, and width of twenty feet, it is still in a state of perfect repair, whereas in many western districts along the Gobi frontier, as here before us, it is little more than an earthen rampart about fifteen feet in height, while for considerable distances, as along the road from Su-chou to Kan-chou, it has entirely disappeared for miles at a stretch. Both the gate and the wall at this point had been recently repaired. We could now see it rising and falling in picturesque undulations as far as the Tibetan ranges. There it stops altogether, after a westward course of over fifteen hundred miles. In view of what was before us, we could not but smile as we thought of that French abbé who undertook, in an elaborate volume, to prove that the "Great Wall of China" was nothing more than a myth.

We were now past another long anticipated land-mark, and before us, far down in the plain, lay the city of Su-chou, which, as the terminal point of the Chinese telegraph-line, would bring us again into electric touch with the civilized world. But between us and our goal lay the Edzina river, now swollen by a recent freshet. We began to wade cautiously through with luggage and wheels balanced on our shoulders. But just at that moment we perceived, approaching from the distance, what we took to be a mounted Chinese mandarin, and his servant leading behind him two richly caparisoned and riderless horses. At sight of us they spurred ahead, and reached the opposite bank just as we passed the middle of the stream. The leader now rose in his stirrups, waved his hat in the air and shouted, in clear though broken English, "Well, gentlemen, you have arrived at last!" To hear our mother tongue so unexpectedly spoken in this out-of-the-way part of the world, was startling. This strange individual, although clad in the regular mandarin garb, was light-complexioned, and had an auburn instead of a black queue

RIDING BY THE GREAT WALL ON THE ROAD TO SU-CHOU.

dangling from his shaven head. He grasped us warmly by the hand as we came dripping out of the water, while all the time his benevolent countenance fairly beamed with joy. "I am glad to see you, gentlemen," he said. "I was afraid you would be taken sick on the road ever since I heard you had started across China. I just got the news five minutes ago that you were at Kiayu-kuan, and immediately came out with these two horses to bring you across the river, which I feared would be too deep and swift for you. Mount your ponies, and we will ride into the city together."

It was some time before the idea flashed across our minds that this might indeed be the mysterious Ling Darin about whom we had heard so much. "Yes," said he, "that is what I am called here, but my real name is Splingard." He then went on to tell us that he was a Belgian by birth; that he had traveled extensively through China, as the companion of Baron Richthofen, and had thus become so thoroughly acquainted with the country and its people that on his return to the coast he had been offered by the Chinese government the position of custom mandarin at Su-chou, a position just then established for the levying of duty on the Russian goods passing in through the northwest provinces; that he had adopted the Chinese dress and mode of living, and had even married, many years ago, a Chinese girl educated at the Catholic schools in Tientsin. We were so absorbed in this romantic history that we scarcely noticed the crowds that lined the streets leading to the Ling Darin's palace, until the boom of a cannon recalled us to our situation. From the smile on the jolly face beside us, we knew at once whom we could hold responsible for this reception. The palace gates were now thrown open by a host of servants, and in our rags and tatters we rolled at once from the hardships of the inhospitable desert into the lap of luxury.

A surplus is not always so easily disposed of as a deficit — at least we were inclined to think so in the case of our Su-chou diet. The Ling Darin's table, which, for the exceptional occasion, was set in the foreign fashion with knives and forks, fairly teemed with abundance and variety. There was even butter, made from the milk of the Tibetan yak, and condensed milk for our coffee, the first we had tasted since leaving Turkey, more than a year before. The Ling Darin informed us that a can of this milk, which he once presented to Chinese friends, had been mistaken for a face cosmetic, and was so used by the ladies of the family. The lack of butter has led many of the missionaries in China to substitute lard, while the Chinese fry their fat cakes in various oils. The Ling Darin's wife we found an excellent and even artistic cook, while his buxom twin daughters could read and write their own language — a rare accomplishment for a Chinese woman. Being unaccustomed to foreign manners, they would never eat at the same table with us, but would come in during the evening with their mother, to join the family circle and read aloud to us some of their father's official despatches. This they would do with remarkable fluency and intelligence.

As guests of our highly respected and even venerated host, we were visited by nearly all the magistrates of the city. The Ling Darin was never before compelled to answer so many questions. In self-defense he was at last forced to get up a stereotyped speech to deliver on each social occasion. The people, too, besieged the palace gates, and clamored for an exhibition. Although our own clothes had been sent away to be boiled, we could not plead this as an excuse. The flowing Chinese garments which had been provided from the private wardrobe of the Ling Darin fluttered wildly in the breeze, as we rode out through the city at the appointed hour. Our Chinese shoes, also, were constantly slipping off, and as we raised the foot to readjust them, a shout went up from the crowd for what they thought was some fancy touch in the way of riding.

From the barrenness of the Gobi to the rank vegetation of the Edzina valley, where the grass and grain were actually falling over from excessive weight, was a most relieving change. Water was everywhere. Even the roadway served in many places as a temporary irrigating-canal. On the journey to Kan-chou we were sometimes compelled to ride on the narrow mud-wall fences that separated the flooded fields of wheat, millet, and sorghum, the prevailing cereals north of the Hoang-ho river. Fields of rice and the opium poppy were sometimes met with, but of the silk-worm and tea-plant, which furnish the great staples

A TYPICAL RECEPTION IN A CHINESE TOWN.

of the Chinese export trade, we saw absolutely nothing on our route through the northern provinces. Apart from the "Yellow Lands" of the Hoang-ho, which need no manure, the arable regions of China seem to have maintained their fecundity for over four thousand years, entirely through the thoughtful care of the peasantry in restoring to the soil, under another form, all that the crops have taken from it. The plowing of the Chinese is very poor. They scarcely do more than scratch the surface of the ground with their bent-stick plows, wooden-tooth drills, and wicker-work harrows; and instead of straight lines, so dear to the eye of a Western farmer, the ridges and furrows are as crooked as serpents. The real secret of their success seems to lie in the care they take to replenish the soil. All the sewage of the towns is carried out every morning at daybreak by special coolies, to be preserved for manure; while the dried herbs, straw, roots, and other vegetable refuse, are economized with the greatest care for fuel. The Chinese peasant offsets the rudeness of his implements with manual skill. He weeds the ground so carefully that there is scarcely a leaf above the ground that does not appertain to the crop. All kinds of pumps and hydraulic wheels are worked, either by the hand, animals, or the wind. The system of tillage, therefore, resembles market-gardening rather than the broad method of cultivation common in Europe and America. The land is too valuable to be devoted to pasture, and the forests nearly everywhere have been sacrificed to tillage to such an extent that the material for the enormously thick native coffins has now to be imported from abroad.

Streams and irrigating-ditches were so frequent that we were continually saturated with water or covered with mud. Our bare arms and legs were so tanned and coated that we were once asked by a group of squalid villagers if "foreigners" ever bathed like themselves. On dashing down into a village, we would produce consternation or fright, especially among the women and children, but after the first onset, giggling would generally follow, for our appearance, especially from the rear, seemed to strike them as extremely ridiculous. The wheel itself presented various aspects to their ignorant fancies. It was called the "flying machine" and "foot-going carriage," while some even took it for the "fire-wheel cart," or locomotive, about which they had heard only the vaguest rumors. Their ignorance of its source of motive power often prompted them to name it the "self-moving cart," just as the natives of Shanghai are wont to call the electric-light "the self-coming moon."

In one out-of-the-way village of northwestern China, we were evidently taken for some species of centaurs; the people came up to examine us while on the wheel to see whether or no rider and wheel were one. We became so harassed with importunities to ride that we were compelled at last to seek relief in subterfuge, for an absolute refusal, we found, was of no avail. We would promise to ride for a certain sum of money, thinking thus to throw the burden of refusal on themselves. But, nothing daunted, they would pass round the hat. On several occasions, when told that eggs could not be bought in the community, an offer of an exhibition would bring them out by the dozen. In the same way we received presents of tea, and by this means our cash expenses were considerably curtailed. The interest in the "foreign horses" was sometimes so great as to stop business and even amusements. A rather notable incident of this kind occurred on one of the Chinese holidays. The flag-decked streets, as we rode through, were filled with the neighboring peasantry, attracted by some traveling theatrical troupe engaged for the occasion. In fact, a performance was just then in progress at the open-air theater close at hand. Before we were aware of it we had rolled into its crowded auditorium. The women were sitting on improvised benches, fanning and gossiping, while the men stood about in listless groups. But suddenly their attention was aroused by the counter attraction, and a general rush followed, to the great detriment of the temporary peddlers'-stands erected for the occasion. Although entirely deserted, and no doubt consumed with curiosity, the actors could not lose what the Chinese call "face." They still continued their hideous noises, pantomimes, and dialogues to the empty seats.

The last fifty miles into Liang-chou, a city founded by a Catholic Chinaman over two hundred years ago, we were compelled to make on foot, owing to an accident

A CHINAMAN'S WHEELBARROW.

that caused us serious trouble all through the remainder of our Chinese journey. In a rapid descent by a narrow pathway, the pedal of one of the machines struck upon a protuberance, concealed by a tuft of grass, snapping off the axle, and scattering the ball-bearings over the ground. For some miles we pushed along on the bare axle inverted in the pedal-crank. But the wrenching the machine thus received soon began to tell. With a sudden jolt on a steep descent, it collapsed entirely, and precipitated the rider over the handle-bars. The lower part of the frame had broken short off, where it was previously cracked, and had bent the top bar almost double in the fall. In this sad plight, we were rejoiced to find in the "City under the Shade" the Scotch missionary, Mr. Laughton, who had founded here the most remote of the China Inland Missions. But even with his assistance, and that of the best native mechanic, our repairs were ineffective. At several points along the route we were delayed on this account. At last the front and rear parts of the machine became entirely separated. There was no such thing as steel to be found in the country, no tools fit to work with, and no one who knew the first principles of soldering. After endeavoring to convince the native blacksmiths that a delicate bicycle would not stand pounding like a Chinese cart-wheel, we took the matter into our own hands. An iron bar was placed in the hollow tubing to hold it in shape, and a band of telegraph wire passed round from front to rear, along the upper and lower rods, and then twisted so as to bring the two parts as tightly together as possible. With a waddling frame, and patched rear-wheel describing eccentric revolutions, we must have presented a rather comical appearance over the remaining thousand miles to the coast.

Across the Yellow Hoang-ho, which is the largest river we encountered in Asia, a pontoon bridge leads into the city of Lan-chou-foo. Its strategical position at the point where the Hoang-ho makes its great bend to the north, and where the gateway of the West begins, as well as its picturesque location in one of the greatest fruit-bearing districts of China, makes it one of the most important cities of the empire. On the commanding heights across the river, we stopped to photograph the picturesque scene. As usual, the crowd swarmed in front of the camera to gaze into the mysterious lens. All the missionaries we had met cautioned us against taking photographs in China, lest we should do violence to the many popular superstitions, but the only trouble we ever experienced in this respect was in arousing popular curiosity. We soon learned that in order to get something besides Chinese heads in our pictures it was necessary first to point the

MONUMENT TO THE BUILDER OF A BRIDGE.

camera in the opposite direction, and then wheel suddenly round to the scene we wished to take. As we crossed the river, the bridge of boats so creaked and swayed beneath the rushing rabble, that we were glad to stand once more upon the terra firma of the city streets, which were here paved with granite and marble blocks. As we rode down the principal thoroughfare, amid the usual din and uproar, a well-dressed Chinaman rushed out from one of the stores and grabbed us by the arm. "Do you speak English?"

he shouted, with an accent so like an American, that we leaped from our wheels at once, and grasped his hand as that of a fellow countryman. This, in fact, he proved to be in everything but birth. He was one of that party of mandarins' sons which had been sent over to our country some years ago, as an experiment by the Chinese government, to receive a thorough American training. We cannot here give the history of that experiment, as Mr. Woo related it — how they were subsequently accused of cutting off their queues and becoming denationalized; how, in consequence, they were recalled to their native land, and degraded rather than elevated, both by the people and the government, because they were foreign in their sentiments and habits; and how, at last, they gradually began to force recognition through the power of merit alone. He had now been sent out by the government to engineer the extension of the telegraph-line from Su-chou to Urumtsi, for it was feared by the government that the employment of a foreigner in this capacity would only increase the power for evil which the natives already attributed to this foreign innovation. The similarity in the phrases, *telegraph pole* and *dry heaven*, had inspired the common belief that the line of poles then stretching across the country was responsible for the long-existing drought. In one night several miles of poles were sawed short off, by the secret order of a banded conspiracy. After several decapitations, the poles were now being restored, and labeled with the words, "Put up by order of the Emperor."

In company with the English missionary, Mr. Redfern, while attempting to get out of the city on the way to his mountain home, we were caught in another jam. He counseled us to conceal the weapons we were carrying in our belts, for fear the sight of them should incite the mob to some act of violence. Our own experience, however, had taught us that a revolver in China was worth nothing if not shown. For persistence, this mob surpassed any we had ever seen. They followed us out of the city and over the three miles' stretch to the mission premises, and there announced their intention of remaining indefinitely. Again Mr. Redfern feared some outbreak, and counseled us to re-

TWO PAGODAS AT LAN-CHOU-FOO.

turn to the city and apply to the viceroy himself for protection. This proved a good move. A special exhibition on the palace parade-grounds gained for us the valuable favor of one who was only fourth in rank to the emperor himself. A body-guard of soldiers was furnished, not only during our sojourn in the city, but for the journey to Singan-foo, on which a good reception was everywhere insured by an official despatch sent in advance. In order to secure for us future respect, a small flag with the government stamp and of yellow color was given us to fly by the side of our "stars and stripes." On this was inscribed the title of "The Traveling Students," as well as answers to the more frequent of the common questions—our nationality, destination, and age. The best mechanic in the local cannon-foundry was then ordered to make, at government expense, whatever repairs were possible on our disabled machines. This, however, as it proved, was not much; most of his time was spent in taking measurements and patterns for another purpose. If his intentions have been carried out, Lan-chou-foo is to-day possessed of a "foot-moving carriage" of home production.

Our sojourn in this city is especially associated with the three names of Woo, Choo, and Moo—names by no means uncommon in Chinese nomenclature. We heard of a boy named the abstract numeral, "sixty-five," because his grandfather happened to reach that age on the very day of his birth. Mr. Moo was the local telegraph operator, with whom we, and our friends Woo and Choo, of Shanghai, associated. All operators in the Chinese telegraph system are required to read and write English. The school established for this purpose at Lan-chou we occasionally visited, and assisted the Chinese schoolmaster to hear the recitations from Routledge's spelling-book. He, in turn, was a frequent partaker of our "foreign chows," which our English-speaking friends served with knives and forks borrowed from the missionaries. Lily and bamboo roots, sharks' fins and swallows' nests, and many other Chinese delicacies, were now served in abundance, and with the ever-accompanying bowl of rice. In the matter of eating and drinking, Chinese formality is extreme. A round table is the only one that can be used in an aristocratic household. The seat of honor is always the one next to the wall. Not a mouthful can be taken until the host raises his chop-sticks in the air, and gives the signal. Silence then prevails; for Confucius says: "When a man eats he has no time for talk." When a cup of tea is served to any one in a social party, he must offer it to every one in the room, no matter how many there are, before proceeding to drink himself. The real basis of Chinese politeness seems to be this: They must be polite enough to offer, and you must be polite enough to refuse. Our ignorance of this great underlying principle during the early part of the Chinese journey led us into errors both many and grievous. In order to show a desire to be sociable, we accepted almost everything that was offered us, to the great chagrin, we fear, of the courteous donors.

MISSIONARIES AT LAN-CHOU-FOO.

LI-HUNG-CHANG.
FROM A PHOTOGRAPH SENT TO THE AUTHORS BY THE PRIME MINISTER.

VI

AN INTERVIEW WITH THE PRIME MINISTER OF CHINA

OUR departure from Lan-chou was not, we thought, regretted by the officials themselves, for we heard that apprehension was expressed lest the crowds continuing to collect around the telegraph-office should indulge in a riot. However, we were loath to leave our genial friends for the society of opium-smokers, for we were now in that province of China which, next to Sechuen, is most addicted to this habit. From dusk till bed-time, the streets of the villages were almost deserted for the squalid opium dens. Even our soldier attendant, as soon as the wooden saddle was taken from his sore-backed government steed, would produce his portable lamp, and proceed to melt on his needle the wax-like contents of a small, black box. When of the proper consistency, the paste was rolled on a metal plate to point it for the aperture in the flute-shaped pipe. Half the night would be given to this process, and a considerable portion of the remaining half would be devoted to smoking small pinches of tobacco in the peculiar Chinese water-pipe. According to an official note, issued early in 1882, by Mr. Hart, Inspector-General of Chinese Customs, considerably less than one per cent. of the population is addicted to opium-smoking, while those who smoke it to excess are few. More to be feared is the use of opium as a poison, especially among Chinese women. The government raises large sums from the import duty on opium, and tacitly connives at its cultivation in most of the provinces, where the traders and mandarins share between them the profits of this officially prohibited drug.

This part of the great historic highway on which we were now traveling, between the two bends of the Hoang-ho, was found more extensively patronized than heretofore. Besides the usual caravans of horses, donkeys, and two-wheeled vans, we occasionally met with a party of shaven-headed Tibetans traveling either as emissaries, or as traders in the famous Tibetan sheep-skins and furs, and the strongly-scented bags of the musk-deer. A funeral cortège was also a very frequent sight. Chinese custom requires that the remains of the dead be brought back to their native place, no matter how far they may have wandered during life, and as the carriage of a single body would often be expensive, they are generally interred in temporary cemeteries or mortuary villages, until a sufficient number can be got together to form a large convoy. Mandarins, however, in death as in life, travel alone and with retinue. One coffin we met which rested upon poles supported on the shoulders of thirty-two men. Above on the coffin was perched the usual white rooster, which is supposed to incorporate, during transportation, the spirit of the departed. In funeral ceremonies, especially of the father, custom also requires the children to give public expression to their grief. Besides many other filial observances, the eldest son is in duty bound to render the journey easy for the departed by scattering fictitious paper-money, as spirit toll, at the various roadside temples.

Singan-foo, the capital of the Middle Kingdom, under the Tsin dynasty, and a city of the first importance more

OPIUM-SMOKERS IN A STREET OF TAI-YUEN-FOO.

than two thousand years ago, is still one of the largest places in the empire, being exceeded in population probably by Canton alone. Each of its four walls, facing the cardinal points, is over six miles long and is pierced in

MISSIONARIES AT TAI-YUEN-FOO.

the center by a monumental gate with lofty pavilions. It was here, among the ruins of an old Nestorian church, built several centuries before, that was found the famous tablet now sought at a high price by the British Museum. The harassing mobs gathered from its teeming population, as well as the lateness of the season, prompted us to make our sojourn as short as possible. Only a day sufficed to reach Tong-quan, which is the central stronghold of the Hoang-ho basin, and one of the best defended points in China. Here, between precipitous cliffs, this giant stream rushes madly by, as if in protest against its sudden deflection. Our ferry this time was not the back of a Chinese coolie nor a jolting ox-cart, but a spacious flat-boat made to accommodate one or two vehicles at a time. This was rowed at the stern, like the gondolas of Venice. The mob of hundreds that had been dogging our foot-steps and making life miserable, during our brief stop for food, watched our embarkation. We reached the opposite shore, a mile below the starting-point, and began to ascend from the river-basin to the highlands by an excavated fissure in the famous "yellow earth." This gives its name, not only to the river it discolors, but, from the extensive region comprised, even to the emperor himself, who takes the title of "Yellow Lord," as equivalent to "Master of the World." The thickness of this the richest soil in China, which according to Baron Richthofen is

ENTERING TONG-QUAN BY THE WEST GATE.

nothing more than so much dust accumulated during the course of ages by the winds from the northern deserts, is in some places at least two thousand feet. Much ingenuity has been displayed in overcoming the difficulties offered to free communication by the perpendicular walls of these yellow lands. Some of the most frequented roads have been excavated to depths of from forty to one hundred feet. Being seldom more than eight or ten feet wide, the wheeled traffic is conducted by means of sidings, like the "stations" in the Suez Canal. Being undrained or un-

MONUMENTS NEAR ONE-SHE-CHIEN.

swept by the winds, these walled-up tracks are either dust-beds or quagmires, according to the season; for us, the autumn rains had converted them into the latter. Although on one of the imperial highways which once excited the admiration of Marco Polo, we were now treated to some of the worst stretches we have ever seen. The mountain ascents, especially those stair-like approaches to the "Heavenly Gates" before reaching the Pe-chili plains, were steep, gradeless inclines, strewn with huge upturned blocks of stone, over which the heavy carts were fairly lifted by the sheer force of additional horse-flesh. The bridges, too, whose Roman-like masonry attests the high degree of Chinese civilization during the middle ages, have long since been abandoned to the ravages of time; while over the whole country the late Dungan rebellion has left its countless ruins.

The people of Shan-si province are noted for their special thrift, but this quality we observed was sometimes exhibited at the expense of the higher virtue of honesty. One of the most serious of the many cases of attempted extortion occurred at a remote country town, where we arrived late one evening, after learning to our dismay that one of our remarkably few mistakes in the road had brought us just fifty miles out of the way. Unusually wearied as we were by the cross-country cuts, we desired to retire early. In fact, on this account, we were not so observant of Chinese formality as we might have been. We did not heed the hinted requests of the visiting officials for a moon-light exhibition, nor go to the inn-door to bow them respectfully out. We were glad to take them at their word when they said, with the usual hypocritical smirk, "Now, don't come out any farther." This indiscretion on our part caused them, as well as ourselves, to suffer in the respect of the assembled rabble. With official connivance, the latter were now free, they thought, to take unusual liberties. So far, in our dealings with the Chinese, we had never objected to anything that was reasonable even from the native point of view. We had long since learned the force of the Chinese proverb that, "in order to avoid suspicion you must not live behind closed doors"; and in consequence had always recognized the common prerogative to ransack our private quarters and our luggage, so long as nothing was seriously disturbed. We never objected, either, to their wetting our paper windows with their tongues, so that they might noiselessly slit a hole in them with their exceptionally long finger nails, although we did wake up some mornings to find the panes entirely gone. It was only at the request of the innkeeper that we sometimes undertook the job of cleaning out the inn-yard; but this, with the prevalent superstition about the "withering touch of the foreigner," was very easily accomplished. Nor had we ever shown the slightest resentment at being called "foreign devils"; for this, we learned, was, with the younger generation at least, the only title by which foreigners were known. But on this particular night, our forbearance being quite exhausted, we ejected the intruders bodily. Mid mutterings and threats we turned out the lights, and the crowd as well as ourselves retired. The next morning the usual exorbitant bill was presented by the innkeeper, and, as usual, one half or one third was offered and finally accepted, with the customary protestations about being under-paid. The innkeeper's grumblings incited the crowd which early assembled, and from their whispers and glances we could see that trouble of some kind was brewing. We now hastened to get the wheels into the road. Just then the innkeeper, at the instigation of the crowd, rushed out and grabbed the handle-bars, demanding at the same time a sum that was even in advance of his original price. Extortion was now self-evident, and, remonstrance being of no avail, we were obliged to protect ourselves with our fists. The crowd began to close in upon us, until, with our backs against the adjoining wall, we drew our weapons, at which the onward movement changed suddenly to a retreat. Then we assumed the aggressive, and regained the wheels which had been left in the middle of the road. The innkeeper and his friend now caught hold of the rear wheels. Only by seizing their queues could we drag them away at all, but even then before we could mount they would renew their grasp.

It was only after another direct attack upon them that we were able to mount, and dash away.

A week's journeying after this unpleasant episode brought us among the peanuts, pigs, and pig-tails of the

MONUMENT NEAR CHANG-SHIN-DIEN.

famous Pe-chili plains. Vast fields of peanuts were now being plowed, ready to be passed through a huge coarse sieve to separate the nuts from the sandy loam. Sweet potatoes, too, were plentiful. These, as well as rice balls, boiled with a peculiar dry date in a triangular corn-leaf wrapper, we purchased every morning at daybreak from the pots of the early street-venders, and then proceeded to the local bake-shops, where the rattling of the rolling-pins prophesied of stringy fat cakes cooked in boiling linseed oil, and heavy dough biscuits cleaving to the urn-like oven.

It was well that we were now approaching the end of

our journey, for our wheels and clothing were nearly in pieces. Our bare calves were pinched by the frost, for on some of the coldest mornings we would find a quarter of an inch of ice. Our rest at night was broken for the want of sufficient covering. The straw-heated *kangs* would soon cool off, and leave us half the night with only our thin sleeping-bags to ward off rheumatism.

But over the beaten paths made by countless wheelbarrows we were now fast nearing the end. It was on the evening of November 3, that the giant walls of the great "Residence," as the people call their imperial capital, broke suddenly into view through a vista in the surrounding foliage. The goal of our three-thousand-one-hundred-and-sixteen-mile journey was now before us, and the work of the seventy-first riding day almost ended. With the dusk of evening we entered the western gate of the "Manchu City," and began to thread its crowded thoroughfares. By the time we reached Legation street or, as the natives egotistically call it, "The Street of the Foreign Dependencies," night had veiled our haggard features and ragged garments. In a dimly lighted courtyard we came face to face with the English proprietor of the Hotel de Peking. At our request for lodging, he said, "Pardon me, but may I first ask who you are and where you come from?" Our unprepossessing appearance was no doubt a sufficient excuse for this precaution. But just then his features changed, and he greeted us effusively. Explanations were now superfluous. The "North China Herald" correspondent at Pao-ting-foo had already published our story to the coast.

That evening the son of the United States minister visited us, and offered a selection from his own wardrobe until a Chinese tailor could renew our clothing. With borrowed plumes we were able to accept invitations from foreign and Chinese officials. Polite cross-examinations were not infrequent, and we fear that entire faith in our alleged journey was not general until, by riding through the dust and mud of Legation street, we proved that Chi-

ON THE PEI-HO.

nese roads were not altogether impracticable for bicycle traveling.

The autumn rains had so flooded the low-lying country between the capital and its seaport, Tientsin, that we were obliged to abandon the idea of continuing to the coast on the wheels, which by this time were in no condition to stand unusual strain. On the other hand the house-boat journey of thirty-six hours down the Pei-ho river was a rather pleasant diversion.

Our first evening on the river was made memorable by an unusual event. Suddenly the rattling of tin pans, the tooting of horns, and the shouting of men, women, and children, aroused us to the realization that something extraordinary was occurring. Then we noticed that the full moon in a cloudless sky had already passed the half-way mark in a total eclipse. Our boatmen now joined in the general uproar, which reached its height when the moon

A CHINAMAN SCULLING ON THE PEI-HO.

was entirely obscured. In explanation we were told that the "Great Dragon" was endeavoring to swallow up the moon, and that the loudest possible noise must be made to frighten him away. Shouts hailed the reappearance of the moon. Although our boatmen had a smattering of pidjin, or business, English, we were unable to get a very clear idea of Chinese astronomy. In journeying across the empire we found sufficient analogy in the various provincial dialects to enable us to acquire a smattering of one from another as we proceeded, but we were

INTERVIEW WITH THE PRIME MINISTER OF CHINA 219

now unable to see any similarity whatever between "You makee walkee look see," and "You go and see," or between "That belong number one pidjin," and "That is a first-class business." This jargon has become a distinct dialect on the Chinese coast.

On our arrival in Tientsin we called upon the United States Consul, Colonel Bowman, to whom we had brought several letters from friends in Peking. During a supper at his hospitable home, he suggested that the viceroy might be pleased to receive us, and that if we had no objection, he would send a communication to the *yamen*, or official residence. Colonel Bowman's secretary, Mr. Tenney, who had been some time the instructor of the viceroy's sons, and who was on rather intimate terms with the viceroy himself, kindly offered to act as interpreter. A favorable answer was received the next morning, and the time for our visit fixed for the afternoon of the day following. But two hours before the appointed time a message was received from the viceroy, stating that he was about to receive an unexpected official visit from the *phantai*, or treasurer, of the Pe-chili province (over which Li-Hung-Chang himself is viceroy), and asking for a postponement of our visit to the following morning at 11 o'clock. Even before we had finished reading this unexpected message, the booming of cannon along the Pei-ho river announced the arrival of the *phantai's* boats before the city. The postponement of our engagement at this late hour threatened to prove rather awkward, inasmuch as we had already purchased our steamship tickets for Shanghai, to sail on the *Fei-ching* at five o'clock the next morning. But through the kindness of the steamship company it was arranged that we should take a tug-boat at Tong-ku, on the line of the Kai-ping railroad, and overtake the steamer outside the Taku bar. This we could do by taking the train at Tientsin, even as late as seven hours after the departure of the steamer. Steam navigation in the Pei-ho river, over the forty or fifty miles' stretch from Tientsin to the gulf, is rendered very slow by the sharp turns in the narrow stream — the adjoining banks being frequently struck and plowed away by the bow or stern of the large ocean steamers.

When we entered the consulate the next morning, we found three palanquins and a dozen coolies in waiting to convey our party to the viceroy's residence. Under other circumstances we would have patronized our "steeds of steel," but a visit to the "biggest" man in China had to be conducted in state. We were even in some doubt as to the propriety of appearing before his excellency in

SALT HEAPS AT THE GOVERNMENT WORKS AT TONG-KU.

bicycle costume; but we determined to plead our inability to carry luggage as an excuse for this breach of etiquette.

The first peculiarity the Chinese notice in a foreigner is his dress. It is a requisite with them that the clothes must be loose, and so draped as to conceal the contour of the body. The short sack-coat and tight trousers of the foreigner are looked upon as certainly inelegant, if not actually indecent.

It was not long before we were out of the foreign settle-

WINDMILLS AT TONG-KU FOR RAISING SALT WATER.

ment, and wending our way through the narrow, winding streets, or lanes, of the densely populated Chinese city. The palanquins we met were always occupied by some high dignitary or official, who went sweeping by with his usual vanguard of servants, and his usual frown of excessive dignity. The fact that we, plain "foreign devils," were using this mode of locomotion, made us the objects of considerable curiosity from the loiterers and passers-by, and in fact had this not been the case, we should have felt rather uncomfortable. The unsympathetic observation of mobs, and the hideous Chinese noises, had become features of our daily life.

The *yamen* courtyard, as we entered, was filled with empty palanquins and coolie servants waiting for the different mandarins who had come on official visits. The *yamen* itself consisted of low one-story structures, built in the usual Chinese style, of wood and adobe brick, in a quadrangular form around an inner courtyard. The common Chinese paper which serves for window-glass had long since vanished from the ravages of time, and the finger-punches of vandals. Even here, at the *yamen* of the prime minister of China, dirt and dilapidation were evident on every hand. The anteroom into which we were ushered was in keeping with its exterior. The paper that covered the low walls and squatty ceiling, as well as the calico covering on the divans, was soiled and torn. The room itself was filled with mandarins from various parts of the country, waiting for an audience with his excellency. Each wore the official robe and dish-pan hat, with its particular button or insignia of rank. Each had a portly, well-fed appearance, with a pompous, dignified mien overspreading his features. The servant by whom we had sent in our Chinese visiting-cards returned and asked us to follow him. Passing through several rooms, and then along a narrow, darkened hallway, we emerged into an inner courtyard. Here there were several servants standing like sentinels in waiting for orders; others were hurrying hither and thither with different messages intrusted to their care. This was all there was to give to the place the air of busy headquarters. On one side of the courtyard the doors of the "foreign reception" room opened. Through these we were ushered by the liveried servant, who bore a message from the viceroy, asking us to wait a few moments until he should finish some important business.

The foreign reception-room in which we were now sitting was the only one in any official residence in the empire, and this single instance of compliance with foreign customs was significant as bearing upon the attitude toward Western ideas of the man who stands at the head of the Chinese government. Everything about us was foreign except a Chinese divan in one corner of the room. In the middle of the floor stood a circular sofa of the latest pattern, with chairs and settees to match, and at one end a foreign stove, in which a fire had been recently lighted for our coming. Against the wall were placed a full-length mirror, several brackets, and some fancy work. The most interesting of the ornaments in the room were portraits of Li-Hung-Chang himself, Krupp the gun-maker, Armstrong the ship-builder, and the immortal "Chinese Gordon," the only foreigner, it is said, who has ever won a spark of admiration from the Chinese people.

While we were waiting for the viceroy, his second son, the pupil of Mr. Tenney, came in and was introduced in the foreign fashion. His English was fluent and correct. He was a bright, intelligent lad of nineteen years, then about to take his first trial examinations for the Chinese degree of scholarship, which, if attained, would make him eligible for official position. Although a son of the viceroy he will have to rise by his own merit.

Our conversation with the viceroy's son extended over ten or fifteen minutes. He asked many questions about the details of our journey. "How," said he, "could you get along without interpreter, guide, or servant, when every foreigner who goes even from here to Peking has to have them?" He questioned us as to whether or not the Chinese had ever called us names. We replied that we usually traveled in China under the *nom de Chinois*, *yang queedza* (the foreign devils), alias *yeh renn* (the wild men). A blush overspread his cheeks as he said: "I must apologize for my countrymen; I hope you will excuse them, for they know no better." The young man expressed deep interest in America and American institutions, and said if he could obtain his father's consent he would certainly make a visit to our country. This was the only son then at home with the viceroy, his eldest son being minister to Japan. The youngest, the viceroy's favorite, was, it was said, the brightest and most promising. His death occurred only a few months before our arrival in Tientsin.

We were holding an animated conversation when the viceroy himself was announced. We all stood to show our respect for the prime minister whom General Grant included among the three greatest statesmen of his day. The viceroy was preceded by two body-servants. We stood before a man who appeared to be over six feet in height, although his head and shoulders were considerably bent with age. His flowing dress was made of rich colored silk, but very plain indeed. Any ornamentation would have been a profanation of the natural dignity and stateliness of Li-Hung-Chang. With slow pace he walked into the room, stopped a moment to look at us, then advanced with outstretched hand, while a faint smile played about his features and softened the piercing glance of his eyes. He shook our hands heartily in the foreign fashion, and without any show of ceremony led the way into an adjoining room, where a long council-table extended over half the length. The viceroy took the arm-chair at the head, and motioned us to take the two seats on his left, while Mr. Tenney and the viceroy's son sat on his right. For almost a minute not a word was said on either side. The viceroy had fixed his gaze intently upon us, and, like a good general perhaps, was taking a thorough survey of the field before he opened up the cannonade of questions

INTERVIEW WITH THE PRIME MINISTER OF CHINA

that was to follow. We in turn were just as busily engaged in taking a mental sketch of his most prominent physical characteristics. His face was distinctly oval, tapering from a very broad forehead to a sharp pointed

FURNACE FOR BURNING WASTE PAPER BEARING WRITTEN CHARACTERS.

chin, half-obscured by his thin, gray "goatee." The crown of his head was shaven in the usual Tsing fashion, leaving a tuft of hair for a queue, which in the viceroy's case was short and very thin. His dry, sallow skin showed signs of wrinkling; a thick fold lay under each eye, and at each end of his upper lip. There were no prominent cheek-bones or almond-shaped eyes, which are so distinctively seen in most of the Mongolian race. Under the scraggy mustache we could distinguish a rather benevolent though determined mouth; while his small, keen eyes, which were somewhat sunken, gave forth a flash that was perhaps but a flickering ember of the fire they once contained. The left eye, which was partly closed by a paralytic stroke several years ago, gave him a rather artful, waggish appearance. The whole physiognomy was that of a man of strong intuition, with the ability to force his point when necessary, and the shrewd common sense to yield when desiring to be politic.

"Well, gentlemen," he said at last, through Mr. Tenney as interpreter, "you don't look any the worse for your long journey."

"We are glad to hear your excellency say so," we replied; "it is gratifying to know that our appearance speaks well for the treatment we have received in China."

We hope our readers will consider the requirements of Chinese etiquette as sufficient excuse for our failure to say candidly that, if we looked healthy, it was not the fault of his countrymen.

"Of all the countries through which you have passed, which do you consider the best?" the viceroy then asked.

In our answer to this question the reader would no doubt expect us to follow etiquette, and say that we thought China was the best; and, perhaps, the viceroy himself had a similar expectation. But between telling a positive lie, and not telling the truth, there is perhaps sufficient difference to shield us from the charge of gross inconsistency. We answered, therefore, that in many respects, we considered America the greatest country we had seen. We ought of course to have said that no reasonable person in the world would ever think of putting any other country above the Celestial Empire; our bluntness elicited some surprise, for the viceroy said:

"If then you thought that America was the best why did you come to see other countries?"

"Because until we had seen other countries," we replied, "we did not know that America was the best." But this answer the viceroy evidently considered a mere subterfuge. He was by no means satisfied.

"What was your real object in undertaking such a peculiar journey?" he asked rather impatiently.

"To see and study the world and its peoples," we answered; "to get a practical training as a finish to a theoretical education. The bicycle was adopted only because we considered it the most convenient means of accomplishing that purpose."

The viceroy, however, could not understand how a man should wish to use his own strength when he could travel on the physical force of some one else; nor why it was that we should adopt a course through central Asia and northwestern China when the southern route through India would have been far easier and less dangerous. He evidently gave it up as a conundrum, and started out on another line.

"Do you consider the Shah of Persia a powerful monarch?" was his next question.

"Powerful, perhaps, in the Oriental sense," we replied, "but very weak in comparison with the Western nations. Then, too, he seems to be losing the power that he does have—he is compelled to play more and more into the hands of the Russians."

"Do you think that Russia will eventually try to take possession of Persia?" the viceroy interrupted.

"That, of course, is problematical," we answered, with the

embarrassment men of our age might feel at being instigated to talk politics with a prime minister. "What we do know, for certain, is that Russia is now, with her Transcaspian railroad, within about forty miles of Meshed, the capital of Persia's richest province of Khorasan; that she now has a well-engineered and, for a great portion of the way, a macadamized road to that city across the Kopet

MR. LIANG, EDUCATED IN THE UNITED STATES, NOW IN THE SHIPPING BUSINESS.

Dagh mountains from Askabad, the capital of Russian Transcaspia; and that half that road the Persians were rather forcibly invited to construct."

"Do you think," again interrupted the viceroy, whose interest in the Russians now began to take a more domestic turn, "that the Russians would like to have the Chinese province of Ili?"

To this question we might very appropriately have said, "No"; for the reason that we thought Russia had it already. She is only waiting to draw it in, when she feels certain that her Siberian flank is better protected. The completion of the Transsiberian railroad, by which troops can be readily transported to that portion of her dominion, may change Russia's attitude toward the province of Ili. We did not, however, say this to his excellency. We merely replied that we believed Russia was seldom known to hold aloof from anything of value, which she thought she could get with impunity. As she was now sending cart-load after cart-load of goods over the border, through Ili, into northern and western China, without paying a cent of customs duty, while on the other hand not even a leaf of tea or thread of cotton passed over the Russian line from China without the payment of an exorbitant tariff; and as she had already established in Kuldja a postal, telegraph, and Cossack station, it would seem that she does not even now view the province of Ili as wholly foreign to the Russian empire.

At this the viceroy cleared his throat, and dropped his eyes in thoughtful mood, as much as to say: "Ah, I know the Russians; but there is no help for it."

At this point we ventured to ask the viceroy if it were true, as we had been informed, that Russia had arranged a treaty with China, by which she was entitled to establish consuls in several of the interior provinces of the Chinese empire, but he evaded the question with adroitness, and asked:

"Did n't you find the roads very bad in China?"

This question was creditable to the viceroy's knowledge of his own country, but to this subject we brought the very best Chinese politeness we could muster. We said that inasmuch as China had not yet adopted the bicycle, her roads, of course, were not adapted to that mode of locomotion.

The viceroy then asked us to describe the bicycle, and inquired if such a vehicle did not create considerable consternation among the people.

We told him that the bicycle from a Chinese point of view was capable of various descriptions. On the pass-

A CHINESE SEEDING-DRILL.

ports given us by the Chinese minister in London the bicycle was called "a seat-sitting, foot-moving machine." The natives in the interior had applied to it various epithets, among which were *yang ma* (foreign horse), *fei-chay* (flying-machine), *szüdzun chay* (self-moving cart), and others. The most graphic description, perhaps, was given by a Chinaman whom we overheard relating to his neighbors the first appearance of the bicycle in his quiet little village. "It is a little mule," said he, "that you drive by the ears, and kick in the sides to make him go." A dignified smile overspread the viceroy's features.

"Did n't the people try to steal your money?" he next inquired.

"No," we replied. "From our impoverished appearance, they evidently thought we had nothing. Our wardrobe being necessarily limited by our mode of travel, we were sometimes reduced to the appearance of traveling mendicants, and were often the objects of pity or contempt. Either this, or our peculiar mode of travel, seemed to dispel all thought of highway robbery; we never lost even so much as a button on our journey of over three thousand miles across the Chinese empire."

"Did the governors you met treat you well?" he asked; and then immediately added: "Being scholars, were you not subjected to some indignity by being urged to perform for every mandarin you met?"

"By nearly all the governors," we said, "we were treated very kindly indeed; but we were not so certain that the same favors would have been extended to us had we not cheerfully consented to give exhibitions of bicycle riding."

There was now a lull in the conversation. The viceroy shifted his position in his chair, and took another whiff from the long, slender Chinese pipe held to his mouth by one of his body-servants. One whiff, and the pipe was taken away to be emptied and refilled. After a short respite he again resumed the conversation, but the questions he now asked were of a personal nature. We enumerate a few of them, without comment, only for the purpose of throwing some additional light on the character of our questioner.

"About how much did the trip cost you? Do you expect to get back all or more than you spent? Will you write a book?

"Did you find on your route any gold or silver deposits?

"Do you like the Chinese diet; and how much did one meal cost you?

"How old are you? [One of the first questions a Chinese host usually asks his guest.] Are you married? What is the trade or profession of your parents? Are they wealthy? Do they own much land?" (A Chinaman's idea of wealth is limited somewhat by the amount of land owned.)

"Will you telegraph to your parents from Shanghai your safe arrival there?

"Were you not rash in attempting such a journey? Suppose you had been killed out in the interior of Asia, no one would ever have heard of you again.

"Are you Democrats or Republicans?" (The viceroy showed considerable knowledge of our government and institutions.)

"Will you run for any political office in America? Do you ever expect to get into Congress?

"Do you have to buy offices in America?" was the last inquiry.

There was considerable hesitancy on the part of us both to answer this question. Finally we were obliged to admit that sometimes such was the case. "Ah," said the viceroy, "that is a very bad thing about American politics." But in this censure he was even more severe on his own country than America. Referring to ourselves in this connection, the viceroy ventured to predict that we might become so well-known as the result of our journey that we could get into office without paying for it. "You are both young," he added, "and can hope for anything."

During the conversation the viceroy frequently smiled, and sometimes came so near overstepping the bounds of Chinese propriety as to chuckle. At first his reception was more formal, but his interest soon led him to dispense with all formality, and before the close of the interview the questions were rapidly asked and discussed. We have had some experience with examining attorneys, and an extended acquaintance with the American reporter; but we are convinced that for genuine inquisitiveness Li-Hung-Chang stands peerless. We made several attempts

A CHINESE BRIDE.

to take leave, but were interrupted each time by a question from the viceroy. Mr. Tenney, in fact, became fatigued with the task of interpreting, so that many of the long answers were translated by the viceroy's son.

The interview was conducted as nearly as possible in the foreign fashion. We smoked cigarettes, and a bottle of champagne was served. Finally the interview was brought to a close by a health from the viceroy to "Ta-mā-quo" (the great American country).

In conclusion we thanked the viceroy for the honor he

had done us. He replied that we must not thank him at all; that he was only doing his duty. "Scholars," said he, "must receive scholars."

The viceroy rose from his chair with difficulty; the servant took him by the elbows and half lifted him to his feet. He then walked slowly out of the room with us, and across the courtyard to the main exit. Here he shook us heartily by the hand, and bowed us out in the Chinese manner.

Li-Hung-Chang is virtually the emperor of the Celestial Empire; the present "Son of Heaven" (the young emperor) has only recently reached his majority. Li-Hung-Chang is China's intellectual height, from whom emanate nearly all her progressive ideas. He stands to-day in the light of a mediator between foreign progressiveness and native prejudice and conservatism. It has been said that Li-Hung-Chang is really anti-foreign at heart; that he employs the Occidentals only long enough for them to teach his own countrymen how to get along without them. Whether this be so or not, it is certain that the viceroy recognizes the advantages to be derived from foreign methods and inventions, and employs them for the advancement of his country. Upon him rests the decision in nearly all the great questions of the empire. Scarcely an edict or document of any kind is issued that does not go over his signature or under his direct supervision. To busy himself with the smallest details is a distinctive characteristic of the man. Systematic methods, combined with an extraordinary mind, enable him to accomplish his herculean task. In the eastern horizon Li-Hung-Chang shines as the brilliant star of morning that tells of the coming of a brighter dawn.